Personal Notes

Also by Sandra E. Lamb

How to Write It

Personal Notes

rite

Heart

casion

SANDRA E. LAMB

ST. MARTIN'S GRIFFIN
New York

www.stmartins.com

The publishers have generously given permission to use materials from the following copyrighted works:
The Right to Write, by Julia Cameron. Copyright © 1998 by Julia Cameron. Used by permission of Jeremy P. Tarcher, an imprint of Penguin Group (USA). *The Letters of Virginia Woolf: Volume Three: 1923–1928.* Copyright © 1977 by Quentin Bell and Angelica Garnett. Reprinted by permission of Harcourt, Inc. *I Love You, Ronnie: The Letters of Ronald Reagan to Nancy Reagan.* Copyright © 2000 by Ronald Reagan Presidential Foundation. *All the Best, George Bush: My Life and Other Writings,* by George H. W. Bush. Copyright © 1999 by Schuster Adult Publishing Group. *The Best-Loved Poems of Jacqueline Kennedy Onassis,* selected and introduced by Caroline Kennedy. Copyright © 2001 by Caroline Kennedy. *Letters to Children from Beatrix Potter,* collected and introduced by Judy Taylor. Letter to Noel, 8 March 1895: Courtesy of the Pierpont Morgan Library MA2009, reproduced by permission of Frederick Warne & Co. Letter to Freda, Christmas 1901: Courtesy of the Free Library of Philadelphia, reproduced by permission of Frederick Warne & Co. Letter to Mrs. Rebeccah Puddleduck: Owner unknown, reproduced by permission of Frederick Warne & Co. *Ghost Soldiers: The Forgotten Epic Story of World War II's Most Dramatic Mission,* by Hampton Sides. *Editor to Author: The Letters of Maxwell E. Perkins,* edited, selected, and introduced by John Hall Wheelock. *The Letters of Lewis Carroll II,* edited by Morton N. Cohen. Permission to quote granted by A. P. Watt Ltd on behalf of Trustees of the CL Dodgson Estate. *Winston and Clementine: The Personal Letters of the Churchills,* edited by Mary Soames. Permission to quote granted by Curtis Brown on behalf of The Lady Soames.

The Library of Congress has cataloged the hardcover edition as follows:

Lamb, Sandra E.
  Personal notes : how to write from the heart for any occasion / Sandra E. Lamb. — 1st ed.
    p. cm.
  Includes bibliographical references.
  ISBN 0-312-30418-8
  1. Letter writing. 2. Interpersonal relations. 3. English language—Rhetoric. I. Title.
PE1483.L36 2003
395.4—dc21

                                                                                    2003041409

ISBN 978-1-250-02646-0 (trade paperback)

First St. Martin's Griffin Edition: January 2013

10 9 8 7 6 5 4 3 2 1

To Charles, Christopher, Eric, and Jay,
from whom each note
is a special song for the heart

Contents

Acknowledgments

BEFORE I MET my agent, Al Zuckerman, a friend of mine and author-client of his, Lisa P., described him as "a treasure." That he is. And I thank him for his continued patience with me as I continue to struggle at the work of artful expression. Certainly, I owe a deep debt of gratitude to my wonderful editor, Marian Lizzi. Her vision and tireless efforts are responsible for what is good and balanced about this book.

To all those historical giants whose personal notes and letters I reviewed in all those wonderful books that preserve them for us, thank you. And to all my friends and relatives who, through the years, have taken pen and paper to heart to write, you have enriched me. Thank you.

Introduction

SINCE THE PUBLICATION of my book *How to Write It: A Complete Guide to Everything You'll Ever Write*, I've been overwhelmed by the positive response I've received from people who want a little help in writing. Of special interest have been the chapters on writing personal notes. There is a genuine hunger to be touched by and connected to others through the simple act of sending, and receiving, personal handwritten notes. During an interview with *The Denver Post*, for example, one editor said, "I wanted *more* personal notes, and so did several other editors who read the book." They said they wanted more examples of those *really* tough-to-write notes like apologies, condolences, and refusals.

Why?

We've all become too busy to write personal notes. They take time; and, if done properly and well, they require a true expression of our inner feelings, our emotions. Personal notes are, perhaps, an index and expression of the heart and soul. And we've grown unaccustomed to exposing ourselves—to others, and even to ourselves—in such an illuminating light.

Our grandparents wrote perhaps three times as many thank-you notes, appreciation notes, congratulations notes, thinking-about-you notes, and just-a-hello notes as we write.

Here's a typical present-day story I've heard many, many variations on. This particular one came from my friend Jenny. For the past twenty years, she has created hand-crafted gifts for her nieces and nephews. As each has married, then started a family, the number of people on her gift list has grown from the original seven to fifty-two, the oldest forty-two years old. Jenny's task has become enormous. Recently, she related that she has *yet* to receive that first thank-you note from even one of these family members.

We need to reestablish the value and art of writing, and we should teach our children to do it, too. We need to help them express themselves to others on paper.

Ironically, our mobile, electronic society of instant communications too often leaves us feeling isolated. We suffer from a universal and growing failure to *really* connect with others—to really create those "human moments."

No woman—no matter how hard she may try—is an island. In fact, most of us do poorly in isolation. Words like lonely, disconnected, desolate, and depressed come to mind. We all need to connect to others. This book will show you how.

There is something very emotional, and very human, that happens to us in the act of taking a pen in hand and writing our thoughts on paper. It is an act that can't be electronically duplicated. The weight and import of a message are far greater when it comes in handwritten form, as is the pleasure that comes from writing it.

Writing is therapy. It can keep us sane; it keeps us connected to our inner feelings, our inner selves. We are because we write!

Personal Notes was written to encourage you to experience and process your own feelings, in your own way. My hope is that it will help you to connect with the people in your life through writing what's in your heart, and that your personal notes will encourage others to pick up a pen and paper, bringing us closer to our loved ones, and ourselves.

Now join your hands
and with your hands your hearts.
—WILLIAM SHAKESPEARE

PART ONE

Before You Write

1

The Power to Connect

We should write because it is human nature to write. Writing claims our world. It makes it directly and specifically our own. We should write because humans are spiritual beings and writing is a powerful form of prayer and meditation, connecting us both to our own insights and to a higher and deeper level of inner guidance.

We should write because writing brings clarity and passion to the act of living. Writing is sensual, experiential, grounding. We should write because writing is good for the soul. We should write because writing yields us a body of work, a felt path through the world we live in.

We should write, above all, because we are writers, whether we call ourselves that or not.

—JULIA CAMERON,
The Right to Write

WHAT'S SO OFTEN MISSING from our lives today is the richness of shared humanity, those moments when we feel really connected to other human beings. The act of writing personal notes not only feeds our own soul, but also lets us share ourselves with others—offering hope, affirming life, connecting.

But let's clarify. Although we have the great advantage of advanced technologies and electronic gadgets that keeps us instantly and constantly in touch, we often feel a deep void that can only be filled when we take a moment to reflect, experience, and reach out to another. Ironically, this can come from something as old-fashioned and simple as writing a personal note.

You may argue that we no longer have any need to handwrite personal notes since we can pick up the telephone, zip off a message by fax, or even more quickly, with a few strokes on the keyboard, zap it to someone by e-mail. But these great modes of communication *don't*, in fact, replace our need for the handwritten personal note. Rather, they underscore the value and function of writing notes by hand.

Why?

Instant communications allow us to function too close to the surface, writing on the run from only that top, thin layer of our thoughts; responding without going deeper, opening our inner well, or drawing out that flow of spirit and words that will really *connect* us to another.

Yes, it's possible to just skim the surface in writing our personal communications, and there certainly is a time and place for that. We don't need to put a lot of heart into an RSVP for every office party, for example.

But to make a real and personal *connection* with another, to share a bit of your humanity, you will want to get in touch with your inner, deeper self. Amazingly, something wonderful will happen. You will nurture your own soul, in addition to touching that of another.

Time and Place

THERE ARE TWO KEYS to any kind of writing: time and place. Often they are inseparable. The right time for writing is when you are closest to your emotional response. In the case of a gift received, that's usually after you've opened it and are basking in the initial delight. If you're not delighted, the right time may be after you've reflected on it for a while. (Reflecting, in any case, is always good.)

Place can be physical and emotional. It may be an inner "click" that signals that you've tuned into your heart, your writing place. A physical place where you love to write is also very helpful. Many creative and very productive writers attest that it's crucial to set the stage by returning to a familiar writing place, with the tools of their trade at the ready. Use both.

A Matter of Focus

TO GET THE FLOW of words started, focus on the person to whom you're writing. Who is she? What do you know about her? What are a few of her favorite things? What is your relationship to her? How does she relate to the subject you're writing about (a kind deed she did, a close relative she has lost, or a party she hosted)?

Now, put yourself and your desire to connect with her into the picture, but keep your thoughts on her and her point of view. Today I went to a neighborhood bookstore for a book signing. Celia, the owner of the little store, had worked extremely hard to make a celebration, a party, for authors. In sitting down to write her a note of thanks, my thoughts ran immediately to how I'd nearly been late because I'd been given erroneous directions by a friend who was also going to the signing. And, of course, I wanted to tell her that I enjoyed the event. Then I stopped, and did what I'm advising here. I began to picture her face as she talked to me during the signing. I asked myself these questions:

Who is she?

What is *her* relationship to the book signing?

How does *she* feel about it?

Something began to move in my heart. I remembered how she'd explained the difficulties she'd had putting the event together, how much work she'd done to get it publicized, and how, if this event didn't generate substantial sales, she'd have to close her store. This book-signing party was her last chance to keep her dream alive.

Entering the Circle of Light

AFTER YOU'VE FOCUSED YOUR THOUGHTS on the recipient, think about the thing itself—the event, gift, gesture, piece of news—you are writing about.

Finally, put yourself and how you feel about your message into what I call a circle of light. Once you have these elements illuminated in your heart, mind, and spirit, you have only to connect the dots, or encircle them—a process that often happens naturally in the outflowing of your expression.

In the case of the bookstore, I put myself back in that moment. When I switched my internal focus from myself to Celia, I immediately stopped thinking about thanking her for hosting the signing or how many books I'd sold. Instead, I began thinking about how she'd confided her experience of putting the event together, and I had access to the connecting flow of words of thanks and encouragement. I also had a couple of ideas to share with her about future events the store might host.

I just finished a thank-you note for a personal gift of a lovely red sweater. Focusing first on the giver, then the gift, and then on how I feel about it, I put my response in order:

Nell,

   You are a marvel at gift-giving. You never, in ten years, have hit one false note. Exactly how do you do it? The red sweater is the perfect size and wonderful with my ski jacket. I wore it to rave reviews on Saturday. Of course you knew it would be great. And it's the perfect answer to what to wear after skiing. I will wear it—I love it—for many enjoyable seasons to come. Nell, thank you, thank you, thank you.

The balancing of these ingredients will change, of course, depending upon the kind of note you are writing. Your heart will tell you. A recent sympathy note I sent to a friend who lost his wife to cancer, for example, made little mention of myself, except to say,

> *... I will always cherish having known Beth, and will continue to return for inspiration, again and again, to the wonderful written body of work she left here for us.*

A Practical Act

LOTS OF "ROUTINE" PERSONAL NOTES can be easily "dashed off" in a few minutes while surrounded by all sorts of external chaos. But there are other notes, especially to your very near and dear, that are served up best after several tries.

I'll often jot down a word or two to get started. Then I'll throw in a few phrases. Usually I'll cross out something I've thought better of, and then try another phrase or two. I usually have a few arrows of reordering and some subpoints, if it is of any length.

It often saves me time, and lets me get to my best and true expression, to use a spiral "personal notes book." If I were really organized—as you may be—I'd keep a spiral notebook exclusively for each category of notes, then next year as Mother's Day approached, I could pull out that notebook and see what I have written to my mother in the past.

So, take your pen and paper, and get ready to create a real human connection.

2

Points of Etiquette
(and Netiquette)

There is always a best way of doing everything, if it be to boil an egg. Manners are the happy ways of doing things.

— *The Conduct of Life (1860)*

USING THE OLD RULES OF ETIQUETTE, I'm sure you'll find, adds value to any event or occasion, or to any social act. Who doesn't like to receive a special, personal, and hand-addressed invitation through the mail, rather than an e-mail or telephone call?

Responding in kind to an invitation or an act of kindness or courtesy is a good general rule; but a better one is making sure your response promotes gentility and civility. While it may be great fun to have an upcoming engagement party listed on a web site, for example, with preparty chatter and anticipation building over several weeks before the event through exchanged e-mails, it's still very nice to maintain the old grace and formality of mailing invitations and responding in the traditional ("snail mail") form.

By the same token, if you receive an invitation to an association luncheon by e-mail, it is certainly proper netiquette to "RSVP" in kind. (*Répondez s'il vous plaît* is French for "please let us know if you are coming.") In fact, e-mail may be the preferred form of response and a courtesy to the sender. Use good manners online, as well as good manners off.

Everything in Its Proper Time

BESIDES RESPONDING IN KIND, remember to respond in *time*. After all, it's a conversation. Just as it's rude not to respond when spoken to, it's rude not to respond when you've received an act of kindness or a gift. Or an invitation. I recently sent out 350 engraved invitations to a semiformal banquet with a request to RSVP. Both an e-mail address and a telephone number were listed. There were sixty acceptances and twelve "regrets." The majority of those invited either did not understand or simply didn't bother to respond.

Sometimes responding in time means waiting. That is often true when your message is high in emotional content. You should allow your note to season before sending. Give it a little time after writing, reread it, and be sure your message reflects your more objective feelings. The time element may be just an hour or two, or it may be a day or two. In the event of a negative or angry response, be sure your pique has passed.

Here are a few time guidelines:

OCCASION OR EVENT   TIMING

INVITATIONS

| Wedding | Send a "Save-the-Date" announcement for those traveling a long distance, or if the wedding is at an especially busy time, four months in advance of the day. |
| | Send out invitations at least |

OCCASION OR EVENT   TIMING

OCCASION OR EVENT	TIMING
Wedding (cont.)	eight weeks before the day, if possible.
Formal Party	Send a formal invitation at least three weeks before the event.
Informal Party	A note helps build anticipation (though invitations may even be made with a telephone call). Something casual and festive in keeping with the spirit of the get-together is best. Give two or three weeks notice, if possible.
Birthday	Tailor the invitations to fit the event, and send them out two to four weeks in advance.
Dinner	Try to issue invitations at least three weeks in advance, especially if the date is during a busy time.
RSVPs	Always respond, as soon as possible, within a day or two. And do it in kind: a formal invitation requires a formal written response; an informal invitation requires an informal one. For regrets, include a thank you

OCCASION OR EVENT   TIMING

RSVPs (cont.)	for the invitation, and mention why you will be unable to attend.

THANK YOUS

Wedding Shower Gift	Friends and family have joined in the celebration to help make this a very special event. Send your note within a week.
Baby Shower Gift	How wonderful to have those who care about your new family. Send your note within a week.
Wedding Gift	Send these as soon as you can manage, and include something personal about how you'll use the gift. All the thank yous should be sent within three months after receiving the gift.
Birth and Adoption Gift	This is a wonderful opportunity to give some special heartfelt news about your new family, and how the gift will be used. You might even include a picture. Send your note within four weeks.

OCCASION OR EVENT   TIMING

Birthday Gifts	Send a thank you within two or three days of receiving the gift.
Christmas, Hanukkah, and Other Gift-Giving Holidays	Send your note within two or three days of receiving the gift.
Formal Party Hostess Gift	Whether you were given flowers, wine, or something else thoughtful, send a personal note right away, within two or three days.
Dinner Party	Being a guest is a very special privilege. Send a thank you right away, but certainly within a few days.
Hospitality	Don't just telephone. Write a thoughtful, sincere note of special thanks, and do it within a couple of days.
Gifts and Acts of Kindness During Illness	Letting those who've shown kindness during your illness know how much you appreciate their caring is vital. Do it as soon as you're up to it.

OCCASION OR EVENT   TIMING

Condolences	For every card, note, bouquet, or act of kindness given after a death, be sure to send a personal note. It's important to acknowledge what the sender said about the deceased in your note. This is a time for remembering and honoring the life of the deceased. Send your notes within six weeks, or as soon as you can.
Referral, Reference, or Recommendation	Send a special and personal note within a day or two. Follow up with another note if, for example, you get the job for which someone recommended you. And determine to do something very nice for the person in return.
Business Gifts, Acts of Kindness, or a Job Well Done	Distinguish yourself as a colleague or business associate with civility and heart, keeping your note consistent with your relationship to the person. Express your appreciation within twenty-four hours.
A Gift Delivered by Mail	Pick up the telephone and let the sender know the item arrived

OCCASION OR EVENT	TIMING
A Gift Delivered by Mail (cont.)	safely. Say a verbal thanks, then within a day, send a handwritten thank you.

Emotional Content

WRITING WITH PASSION CAN be the key that releases a comforting flow to an anguished and grieving parent, like all those thousands of personal notes and letters sent to the families of slain Columbine teens. Such notes of shared emotion can even create a place where two souls meet, commune, and find solace. It is vital at such times of difficulty and grief, however, to keep the focus on the recipient, and to make her support and succor your goal.

Anger is very difficult to handle effectively on the page. While you may very well need to vent your negative emotions, you may find that after you've written them down on paper, you'd best read them aloud (to yourself only), then tear the paper into fine confetti. It's important to temper your response (no pun intended) with fact and objectivity. Don't shoot off a note demanding an apology, for example, before you've given it some shelf time and have given yourself the opportunity to become separated from the heat of your initial emotions. Reread your note after an hour, a few hours, or even twenty-four. You may then think and feel quite differently about the situation and elect to write something very different. If you're still uncertain, read it to an objective friend or a professional who will keep it confidential.

Netiquette: Niceness On Line

E-MAIL DOESN'T SUBSTITUTE for a handwritten note, but it holds some wonderful possibilities. There are many times when an e-mail serves just the right purpose—for example, those quick questions you need an answer to in no particular time frame. It's great for check-ins with friends, colleagues, and associates, and it saves time when something needs to be conveyed immediately.

But it's important to remember, first of all, the personality characteristics e-mail messages may lack. The combined immediacy, intimacy, and anonymity of the Internet can cause you to fracture a relationship in a nanosecond. Always use the best of e-manners to avoid being labeled one who flames others. Try to give every message lots of leeway in the offense department. And remember, the little emoticons, like smiley faces, winks, and little shocked expressions, don't effectively put a happy face on an insult.

If your message requires a *human moment*, that is, if it is high in either emotional or personal content, e-mail is not the proper vehicle. If it requires dialogue or negotiation, or if the content is of a personnel, confidential, or financial nature, don't use e-mail. Use a face-to-face exchange when these elements are present.

Pick up the telephone when you need an immediate answer from someone with whom you don't share instant e-mail messaging. Leave a voice message if the person you want to communicate with prefers voice contact, or if your message will benefit from the nuance of voice inflection. (E-mails aren't for everyone. Often the age of your recipient will give you a clue about receptivity. Ask if in doubt.) Sending an e-message festooned with those emoticons won't change your recipient's mind about an angry or critical message. Use emoticons only if you know her well, and know she enjoys them. Many people view them as cryptic, silly, or insultingly simplistic.

Always send a handwritten message when you want to offer a personal word of praise, comfort, or support, because writing it down adds the weight of care, contemplation, and a permanent record.

Make sure your life in cyberspace is rich with great interpersonal rewards. A few additional considerations may help: (1) Remember the nature of e-mail is casual (it's dress-down Friday at the office), more informal than an interoffice memo. (2) Use it when time is crucial, when you're addressing a large group, and when no one concerned will require or want a permanent record.

Responding

THE WRITTEN RSVP is an endangered species. Before we completely do away with this gracious act of civility, let's consider how valuable it is. From the French "*Répondez s'il vous plaît*," RSVP literally means "respond, if you please." Today the term refers to letting a host know whether you will or will not be attending an event.

Social observers report increasing abuses of the RSVP: (1) invitees respond, stating that they will attend, then don't; (2) invitees respond that they will attend, put in a cursory appearance, then leave early; (3) invitees don't respond at all, then put in an appearance. Whatever the excuses, all of these infractions are not only rude, they create a huge problem for the hostess, and can seriously damage the gala spirit of an event.

Here are the rules: (1) RSVP within a day or two of receiving an invitation; (2) if faced with more than one invitation for the time frame, select one and send your regrets to the other(s), unless it is something like an open house that has no strict time constraints (if this is the case, ask the hostess if this is acceptable); (3) don't RSVP that you'll attend, then decide not to. If a true emergency arises and you are unable to attend, contact the hostess as soon as possible, and write a personal note of explanation and apology as soon as you can.

Regrets

WHEN YOU RECEIVE AN INVITATION and cannot accept, respond in kind with your regrets. In the case of a formal wedding or gala event, a reply card will be enclosed that will make this task a simple matter of filling in the proper blank. When you can't make it after you've said you'll be there, or when you were out of town and completely missed the window of proper response time, you will want to call and send a personal note of explanation and regret. In any case, your personal note will promote good will and add to the celebration, so use your note to offer best wishes.

3

Tools of the Trade

You write it all, discovering it at the end of the line of words. The line of words is a fiber optic, flexible as wire; it illumines the path just before its fragile tip. You probe with it, delicate as a worm.

—ANNIE DILLARD

To Clive Bell

Hogarth House, Paradise Road
Richmond, Surrey

February 1923
Dearest Clive,

I have to see my sister on Thursday, and should come round too late for a prolonged and animated conversation: so why shouldn't you come here on Friday or Saturday: or why shouldn't I come to tea with you on Tuesday?

Please settle one or t'other.

I can't face your blasted telephone, which kicks in my ear like an infuriated mule.

Yours
V.W.
[Virginia Woolf]

IMAGINE OUR FOREMOTHERS functioning as family social secretaries from their command centers of high-gloss mahogany desks with delicately curved legs, which stood in the corner of that special room, the library, as Scarlett O'Hara remembers her mother in *Gone with the Wind*. Or, perhaps that command center was in a cozy niche off the master bedroom suite nestled in a quiet, sunny corner. Perhaps these women, like Elizabeth Barrett Browning, may have used a hand-tooled, leather-topped lap desk while travelling or resting, outfitted with all the essentials for the job, from a cut-glass ink bottle to a score of fancy quill pens and cottony paper. In writing those beautiful, thoughtful letters and notes in their own lovely penmanship, I can nearly see them take up their quill pens, dip them into a deep, little well of India ink, and pour out whatever was in their hearts and on their minds.

And certainly no self-respecting lady would have been without her supply of personalized notepaper and envelopes. If they could afford it, these were probably of rich vellum or feathery cotton, and reflected their own personalities.

After writing they would have carefully checked to see that the ink was dry, perhaps blotting it or fanning it. Then they'd apply stamps kept in a little cubbyhole or drawer. It was a lovely ritual and tradition, and they played the vital role of keeper of the civil and social soul of the family.

Men wrote too, of course. But it seems that caring for the family's social well-being, the function of many of those notes, became primarily a woman's work. Now with every family member so busy, it's wise to divide this function.

Correspondence can be made easy and special today, as it was in times past. One way is to keep a supply of stationery and notecards at home and at the office. That way, immediately after a luncheon, for example, you can write a thank-you note to the hostess while the event is fresh in your mind.

Consider purchasing your own special stationery, too, and personalize it with a monogram-embossing tool, or add a sealing wax stamped with your own seal. Even a telltale hint of your special pot-pourri can be achieved by storing the paper in a drawer or box with some fragrant dried blossoms. You'll undoubtedly want to have your stationery in a couple of sizes and types. For general short notes, you'll want sheets of notepaper about 5" by 7" or 4" by 6". You will also want a supply of fold-over cards of heavier weight, called card stock, to use for thank yous.

For special responses, like thank yous for wedding gifts, select sta-tionery that is consistent with the formality of your wedding invita-tions. Other options for wedding thank yous include cards with a wedding picture inserted into the front, which makes a nice keep-sake. (Some couples are placing disposable cameras on wedding din-ner guest tables and are enclosing a guest photo with their thank you.)

For a formal wedding, use traditional thank you "informal" notes, 4" by 5", that match your wedding invitation stock. These can be ordered with your invitations in an appropriate weight, and can be printed with names or a monogram on the front. You can then continue to use them for personal notes.

Things like fine paper, lined envelopes, monograms, embossing, and stenciling can make your notes even more special—though they are by no means required.

Personalized notecards are often useful, too. When I recently asked an author what kind of special gift she'd really appreciate for speaking to a group of writers, she responded without hesitation that a bookstore had given her a cache of small, 4" by 5" embossed note-cards with only her name on them. "I find these ever so useful, and elegant," she said. Create some for yourself. You'll be amazed how useful they can be.

PART TWO

Notes of Thanks, Hope, and Joy

4

Thank You

Remember to be thankful.
—ANONYMOUS

Dearest Pia,

What a delightful dinner party! Only you could create such a wonderful occasion as a repeat "New Moon Feast." And with such an interesting and eclectic group of people. How did you possibly know we should all be friends?

Now that we've attended our third, I must tell you each gets better. It has truly enriched our lives, having new and deeper connections to Jared, Rick, Madison, David, Jim, and Alexis. How we look forward to each new moon (we're even following the lunar calendar now), and to learning what has happened in each person's life.

Thank you, thank you, thank you for including us, and for bringing all your ingenuity and generosity to this wonderful occasion.

Fondly,
Susan and Nigel

THANK-YOU NOTES HAVE BECOME an endangered species. And, in some families, virtually extinct.

It's ever so true that if you want a friend—or a brother, or a sister—you must be one. Keeping connected to others does mean making an effort. There's always time enough to express thanks for a gift or act of kindness. It's exercising your thank-you muscles.

In addition, the simple act of sitting down and writing out a personal note in longhand can start to open up that well of creativity within you. And it means that you're the first one to experience that wonderful outpour from your heart. Then it flows on to the person you're writing to.

Being thankful and expressing it doesn't require a huge amount of time, an extraordinary wit, or even an extensive vocabulary. It just requires getting in touch with your own thankfulness and expressing it. Here are some simple steps that will get you there.

Focus on the Giver

FOCUSING ON THE PERSON who originated the act of kindness puts everything into proper perspective. You might even imagine the person in the act of putting together your surprise birthday party, shopping for that college alarm clock, writing that special letter of recommendation, or picking out that book to bring to the hospital after your surgery.

You might start: "Dear Aunt Jenn, only you knew—when I didn't—that I needed to own a green sweatshirt. You're prescient, and the most thoughtful and practical person I know. I know it's not so easy shopping for a guy who owns—and wants to own—only three green shirts. But you did it!" . . .

Name the Gift Early

THIS IS OFTEN A KEY to getting started. It helps you connect the giver and the gift. "The scarf is lovely." "A gift certificate to Amazon is a perfect graduation gift." "The blue crystal parrot is exactly what's been missing from my collection."

This gift emphasis can, of course, have a definite upside or downside. A gift of money, when you've experienced a financial loss, is a godsend. A tangerine sweater, if you have auburn hair and can't wear anything orange (especially since it's two sizes too small), presents a challenge in tactfulness. Nevertheless, you can express thankfulness in both situations. (And when a gift isn't right, it's best to emphasize the giver's thoughtfulness and mention an exchange. The giver, after all, intended to bring joy and give you something useful.)

Dear Joanna,

Imagine our relief, and our joy, when, the day after the house burned—leaving us with the clothes (nightclothes) on our backs—Renee, the children, and I opened your overnight delivery to find your check.

We all cried, as I told you on the telephone. What I didn't get to tell you is what little Annie said later: "Aunt Joanna is our very own guardian angel, isn't she?" (We'd just been reading a bedtime story about a guardian angel the night before the fire.)

Yes, you are, Joanna. Bless you.

We'll be able to get things sorted out now, thanks to your generosity. And we'll have some desperately needed cash until the insurance check comes through on Thursday.

I hope we'll never be called upon to reciprocate in exactly the same situation, but we'll certainly be here whenever, and however, you need a helping hand.

I'll get repayment to you in a month. Your act of kindness is an answer to prayer.

Love,
Gervis

Dear Aunt Rita,

How extremely thoughtful of you to remember my birthday; and even more thoughtful of you to send me the cashmere sweater. You know how I love cashmere.

Since you saw me last summer, I'm sorry to say, my "carrot top" hair has darkened just enough to clash with the sweater's great shade of tangerine. So, I've exchanged it for exactly the same sweater in teal. Here's a picture of me in it. It's great with my white wool skirt, don't you think?

I feel fabulous in it, and it gives me a very special outfit for college. I'll think of you each time I wear it, and appreciate your thoughtfulness.

Your loving niece,
Summer

Connecting the Gift to the Giver

THIS IS USUALLY AN AUTOMATIC reflex that comes out of naming the gift or kindness:

Pat,

You've done it again! Offering to care for our plants when we found—as we were ready to leave on vacation—that the person we'd contracted with to do it was gone on vacation herself. Thank you so much for stepping into the breach. You've proven, again, the true meaning of being a good neighbor.

Please call on us when you take your vacation next month. May we water your plants and cut your lawn?

We hope this "thank you" plant matches the red-and-gold theme in your front yard.

Thank you, Good Neighbor.

Best regards,
Buzz and Bea

You can even use the words of some of the famous thankful hearts to get you started:

I'll never be able to say it as eloquently as Emerson: "A day for toil, an hour for sport, but for a friend is life too short."

John Dryden expressed it so well, "Pains of love be sweeter far than all other pleasures are."

The Chinese proverb, "Sincere words are not that grand," makes room for my humble, heart-felt thank you.

Connect Yourself to the Gift or Act of Kindness

ANY EXPRESSION OF THANKS should connect you to the gift and explain its significance to you. Sometimes this is very simple, like the introduction to a job opportunity you wouldn't have had access to on your own:

Dear David,

To say I'm grateful for your act of kindness in referring me to Avery Reynolds, to be considered for the Executive Director position, is just not adequate. I'm truly thrilled at the opportunity your reference has opened up. And it's all because you were thoughtful and caring enough to make the effort (and to take the risk) of referring me to your friend.

We did meet today as scheduled, and I believe it went extremely well.

Avery (as he instructed I call him) is to get back to me on Monday with details of an offer. I believe we've already established a very exciting job description.

I'll call you and let you know the final outcome. But whatever it is, I shall always be indebted to you for thinking of me, and presenting me with the chance of a lifetime.

There is, of course, no way to repay you. But you've set a wonderful example for me to follow. Be assured your act of kindness will be passed on to another person the very first time I have an opportunity.

Gratefully,
Barry

For the heirloom clock you've never liked, think about what it means in terms of your relationship to the giver. Try focusing on how you will use the gift, or what impact the kindness has had, or will have, on you:

Dear Aunt Rose,

The mantel clock you sent to Henry and me for our wedding has already taken up a place of honor on the living room mantel. Here's a picture of it. Doesn't it look like it belongs there?

Every time I walk by it, I think of you, and cherish your very special thoughtfulness, and your sacrifice in parting with Aunt Lucy's clock. My fondest hope is that it will become a bond between us for many long years to come, and that you will come and visit us, and the clock, often.

Affectionately,
Charity (and Henry)

Connecting Your Feelings about the Gift to the Giver

PERHAPS THE PREVIOUS NOTE demonstrates how well this can work. But sometimes it's not as transparent, or as simple. For the interview that turned out to be a bust, or maybe a complete misfit or misrepresentation, the task is more challenging. But with practice, it gets less daunting.

A word of caution: Don't force or falsify a thank you. It will sound insincere. Rather, remember that by continuing to exercise your thank-you muscles you will begin to recognize the elements in every gift or kind act for which you can honestly be thankful.

When an acquaintance has sent you on a wild goose chase for a job opening, and it turns out to be completely wrong or inappropriate, you'll still want to thank the person for the effort. But you may also want to establish the fact that there was a problem, and maybe even what it was. And you will want to prevent the situation from being repeated. This note to Ralph does both:

Dear Ralph,
  I did meet with Elizabeth Buford as you recommended. It was kind of you to think of me in regard to this new opportunity.

It appears, after a brief discussion, however, that Elizabeth is looking for quite a different set of skills than those I possess, and won't, at any rate, be adding anyone to her staff for at least ten to eighteen months.

This experience has caused me to do a lot of thinking, Ralph, and I've decided I'll stay put for the foreseeable future.

Thank you again for thinking for me. For the present, I'd request that you not mention me as a candidate for any new position.

My best wishes for your continued job search. If I hear of a position that sounds like a fit for you, I'll give you a call.

Sincerely,
Ben

When You Don't Have Anything Nice to Say

ALTHOUGH DOROTHY PARKER IS credited with saying, "When you don't have anything nice to say, come sit by me," it's probably your mother you credit with, "If you don't have anything nice to say, don't say anything at all." In truth, you can always say something nice. And truthful. Or, you can, perhaps, say something that compliments the efforts of the sender; and/or you can nicely say something that *needs* to be said. And if done tactfully, what you write can have the desired effect of letting in some fresh air where it's needed, adding some new insight, and maybe even creating a better relationship.

This is the time to focus on strengthening your connection to the giver (unless it's the rare situation where you don't want the relationship to grow): "Thank you for your efforts in making the initial contact," or, "It was nice of you to refer me, but I won't be pursuing this avenue at this time." "Thanks for your confidence, but due to some sensitive work considerations, I'd request that you not recommend me in the future without checking with me first."

When the dreaded "family heirloom" green dragon soup tureen is sent from Aunt Mary as a wedding gift, you'll need to be tactful, and maybe even creative, in coming up with a way to make the connection more meaningful. It could even be your opportunity to see the gift in a brand new light.

Dear Aunt Mary,

Brent and I want to thank you for selecting us as next keepers of this family treasure, The Dudgeon Soup Dragon.

In trying to find a way to share it with more family members, I'm thinking that it would be so nice to create a history of it, with soup recipes and the occasions on which they were served. Then we can all share these remembrances, and pass them on to the next generation.

Would you please write down as much of its history as you can remember, and also the family soups you remember being served for particular occasions? Once I receive your input, I'll send it around to Aunt Lois, Aunt Wilda, and Aunt Barbara. Then I'll put all the responses together in a family history and recipe book. (I know Grandmother has quite a few photos, too, that will be wonderful to include.)

I'll be storing the The Dragon at Mom's, since Brent and I have a closet of an apartment. We're looking forward to Christmas when we'll all use it together. Which soup recipe would you recommend for Christmas Eve? What about the fresh creamed mushroom?

Your niece,
Julia Dudgeon (and Brent Noss)

The secret in such situations is to focus on the positive, and your intent to elevate your connection.

Imagine your brother has invited you and your husband for the weekend, then announced—at the last minute—that you'll need to stay at a nearby hotel. When you arrive, he leaves you sitting at the airport for two hours before he sends his assistant to pick you up and take you to the hotel.

You won't feel like thanking him. Especially if he and his wife then leave you whiling away hours in the hotel room waiting for message updates, which change—with each call—his prearrangement for your time to get together. So, what do you say?

First, allow yourself to vent by writing out any anger or frustration you feel. Read your message aloud (only to yourself, of course), breathe deeply, then tear it into tiny pieces and throw it away. When you're calm, start over with something like:

Dear Susan and Eric,

It was great to see you this weekend. The time we were able to spend together was wonderful, but all too brief. We simply don't see enough of each other, and I'd like to suggest we work on correcting that.

Since we've both expressed interest in having the dude ranch experience, how about meeting in Durango in August to do just that? I'll send a listing of Web sites for you to take a look at, and I'll get the advice of my friend, who has visited all of the ranches for a book he's writing on the subject.

Thanks for making the reservations for this weekend, and for putting other details together. Next time we'll meet somewhere without interruptions and do a complete get-away. What fun! We're looking forward to it already.

With love,
Willie and Jan

When to Send a Note Isn't Enough— Creating a Bold New Way

WHEN YOU'VE RECEIVED a random act of kindness, repay it in kind. If an act or a gift is of such magnitude that a simple written thank you isn't adequate, be creative in coming up with an expression of thanks—though the written one should be part of it—that is in keeping with the spirit and dimensions of the gift or act.

When friends have given you the use of their cottage on the lake for a week, and their anniversary happens to be coming up, for example, you are presented with a great opportunity. You may not be able to reciprocate in like monetary value, but perhaps you can in thoughtfulness.

Why not create your own unique anniversary greeting as part of your thank you? Maybe it's a special sonnet about how they met, and how they enjoy their life together. You know that your attempt to create a special one-of-a-kind greeting is just the thing to commemorate their sixth anniversary.

And maybe the three of you share a love for Gregorian chants, or mandolin music. Or cello solos. There may be just the right creative combination available for you to bring together one of life's truly memorable events. Use your imagination.

Putting your creative energy into a gift idea is bound to produce something very special:

> *Dear Alicia,*
>
> *I should have suspected that the same person who orchestrated that wonderful anniversary surprise, a serenade outside our window while we vacationed in Paris, would be capable of arranging a surprise birthday mud bath in my hotel in New York. How did you know that it would perform the very exhilarating magic that*

would catapult me out of my blue funk at having to spend my
birthday alone, on a business trip?

You are truly a marvel! The best friend anyone could have.

Just wait until it's your birthday! I'm going to be staying up
nights trying to think up something just a fraction as special.

Thank you, Girlfriend!

Love, Sophie

A Word in Time

RESPONDING ON TIME is important; but more important is
responding. So, if you've procrastinated, 'fess up with something
brief, then focus on the thank you. To deemphasize the tardiness,
you'll usually want to put it in the second paragraph; but sometimes
it's best right up front.

Dear Shelly and Bill,

Forgive us for such a tardy note in response to your wonderful,
yellow terry sleepers for Raphael. Our lateness doesn't mean we
don't love the sleepers. They're perfect. (In fact, we've enclosed a
photo of him in them, so you can see for yourself.) Our problem is
just that our after-baby life is still running way behind schedule.

How very thoughtful of you. You made a wonderful choice.
We think he'll be able to wear the sleepers for another few months.

In loving thanks,

Rhoda, Gary, and Raphael

Remember, it's never too late to be thankful. And you can't do it
any sooner. So do it now.

Sorrow and Thank Yous

AFTER A DEATH OR a very serious illness in the family, you may want to appoint someone to send out a prepared note indicating a close family member will respond later:

> *We, the family of William Crow, are sending this note to thank all of you, who so generously rendered many, many acts of kindness in sending flowers, cards, and food, and offering services during William's illness and recent passing.*
>
> *We lost our beloved William far too soon.*
>
> *We so appreciate all your kind thoughts, prayers, and deeds, and will communicate with you individually in the coming weeks.*
>
> *Thank you.*
>
> *The Family of William Crow*

A personal note of thanks after a bereavement should name the item given, express your thanks, and, if possible, make a personal connection between the gift or kindness and the one in whose memory it was offered.

> *Dear Anita and Darryl,*
>
> *Thank you for the lovely red gladiola arrangement you sent to the funeral home after Mom died. You remembered her penchant for glads, especially red ones. Those you sent looked very much like the ones that lined her garden wall each spring, standing as tall, proud, and well-turned out as palace guards.*
>
> *It was so thoughtful of you. We were deeply touched. I'm sure Mom is sitting up there right now retelling all the angels that that spray should have gotten the purple ribbon for blooms and compo-*

sition, just as she did for many years as a judge for the Annual Hartford Flower Show.

Mom loved your visits last year. She wrote several times about your great blueberry pies, and your lively discussions about Civil War heroes.

When I think about her funeral, I picture your gift of red glads. Thank you both.

Gratefully,
Millie and Reed

Dear Devon,

It takes a very special person—one especially tuned in to what's really needed, and one who cares deeply—to sense and know that whatever else, livestock must still be fed, and so must all the people who arrive from out of town when a death in the family occurs.

Thank you, Devon, for stepping in and organizing the feeding of the livestock; and thank you for all the trips you made back and forth.

Dad often said, "If the sun comes up, you can count on Devon." How true, even if it rains. Dad counted you among his closest friends.

Thank you.

Warmest wishes,
Juanita and Juan

No-Occasion Thank Yous

THERE ARE MANY PEOPLE who make our lives so much richer just by doing their jobs in their own very special way, and some by just being who they are. Why not thank them?

When you take the opportunity to show your appreciation for this sort of everyday act of helpfulness or kindness, a wonderful thing happens. You realize the unique principle of appreciating others—the rich overflow that comes from telling someone she is appreciated, amazingly, comes back to *you!*

Dear Pearl Graham,

I needed to write a note of huge thanks to the teacher who has helped create eagerness for learning in our son Jack.

Last year, every morning was a struggle to get Jack ready for school because he didn't want to go. There were statements like, "I hate math," and "I just don't get it." It was a daily parade of long faces and even tears.

Now, only ten weeks into the school year, there are smiles before school, and dinner discussions usually start with statements like, "Guess what I learned today." It's a miracle!

It's often said that adults can probably only name four or five teachers, tops, with whom, throughout their entire academic careers, they felt they had a real connection. I'm certain you'll always be the first on Jack's short list.

Thank you so much. We're so happy you are Jack's teacher this year!

Please let us know when and where you're in need of parent volunteers for class activities.

Respectfully,
Melissa and Darren Ward

Using Humor

WHEN WRITING WITH HUMOR, it's important to know something about the sense of humor of the person to whom you're writing. Still, it's risky. Things written take on more weight, and don't always translate with the nuances you can more easily achieve in a verbal exchange. So, proceed with caution. And remember, it's generally safer to use self-deprecating humor.

If you've been given a humorous house gift when friends arrived for a dinner party, or a humorous birthday gift, sending a thank you that includes a humorous statement will undoubtedly be received in the vein you intended. Otherwise, think carefully about it.

Dear Allie,

The Mickey Mouse watch is marvelous! Only you would think of such an appropriate and delightful gift. I love it!

Now let me review: the small hand refers to the general point in time, and the large hand points to the details. Is that right?

So, when we next agree to meet at a quarter to three, I'll try to make sure Mickey's hands are in that perfectly outstretched position. (I suppose this means there's no more excuse for being late?)

What a marvelous gift. I'll cherish it always.

Love,
Annie

Teach Your Children Well

IT'S NEVER TOO EARLY for your child to see you in the act of being thankful. Start as early as possible, explaining to your child that when Grandma and Grandpa send her something, she'll want to thank them. Right away. It's very easy to direct her through the steps of expressing thankfulness while you write down her words.

As soon as your child begins to print, make it an exciting thing

When to Write

Send a handwritten note of thanks in response to:

- *Gifts* of all kinds, including weddings, showers, birthdays, holidays, anniversaries, and Bar or Bat Mitzvahs
- *Dinner*, party, or other type of get-togethers
- *Condolences and acts of kindness* after a death in the family
- *Business order or contract*
- *Job interview*, or interview of any kind
- *Referrals* of clients, customers, or patients
- *Reference* for position, whether business or personal
- *Hospitality*, either business or personal
- *Contributions* to fundraising activities, events, and drives
- *Membership* into a club, association, or professional organization

Check the guide on pages 9–14 for the timing of each type of note.

you do together, along with, maybe, sending the grandparents a piece of artwork your child has created.

The thankful child is a happy child! And this is a wonderful early step of self-expression, as well as a lesson in how to be connected with, and care for, others.

Hogarth House, Paradise Road,
Richmond, Surrey
Sunday [7 January 1923]

Dear Mrs Nicolson,
   It is extraordinarily good of you to send me Hassan, *and I am ashamed that you should take this trouble, owing to my laziness, for I have meant to get it for ever so long.*
   I shall start reading it and testing my theories of modern poetry directly. I am in a fit state, but having sat up till three this morning watching other people dance, I am sunk in the depths of stupidity.
   I hope you'll come and look at my great aunt's photographs of Tennyson and other people some time. My sister has many of them at her house.

Yours very sincerely
Virginia Woolf

Some Points of Etiquette

- Verbal thank yous for gifts don't substitute for written ones.
- Stay away from general statements; make your thank yous specific.
- Don't let your prose go beyond your true feelings. Flowery insincerity will defeat your purpose. Use, instead, a simple "thank you very much."
- Mentioning the amount of money received as a gift is sometimes considered tactless. If you know the recipient

well, you may conclude that to say, "Thank you, Uncle Joe, for the check for $50," will not offend him. If this is the case, mention it. For others you don't know well, "Thank you for the check" is better.

- In a short note, the use of "Thanks again" is repetitious. Instead, conclude with a sincere, personal compliment.
- *Don't procrastinate.* A late thank you carries with it a ring of insincerity, and must also be explained. Write, and don't belabor your tardiness.
- When a gift was sent collectively by a number of givers, each should be sent a personal written thank you. The exceptions here are when the gift is received by a family, a department, or a club or association. In these cases, address the givers collectively and request that your thank-you note be circulated or posted.

5

Congratulations

Only connect! . . . Only connect the prose and the passion, and both will be exalted, and human love will be seen at its height.

—E. M. FORSTER

I'VE FOUND THAT a true and heartfelt note of congratulations expands the joy of the recipient like yeast raises bread. In fact, I think nothing makes our accomplishments sweeter than other people's recognition, compliments, and praise.

Congratulations! You outdid yourself on that insightful piece on aging. I especially like your comparison to the ginkgo tree. Your writing is truly outstanding, and I was delighted that your piece won the "Best of the Year Award."

Congratulations, I see you are nominated for President of the Aces. You'll be great, and you've got my vote.

Congratulations! You did a wonderful job of getting that paper in on time. I know it took a Herculean effort, and you did it.

Don't wait for a really *big* occasion; recognize "smaller" points of joy that you know are important to the person. Your note will make a long-lasting impression if you follow a few guidelines: keep it simple, sincere, and in tune with your relationship to the recipient. Specific occasions for congratulations like weddings and anniversaries are covered in the following chapters, but there are many other occasions, too, when you may want to recognize someone's good news with a short note:

- *Personal achievements* like making a successful speech, getting an article published, winning an award, winning a sports competition, finishing a marathon, completing a course of study, receiving a prize for a hobby or avocation

- *Family events* like moving into a new house, launching a new business from the home, finishing a course together, or completing a large remodeling project

- *Social events* like being invited to be a member of a club or other group

- *Religious events* like joining a church, ordination, taking vows, or becoming an elder or deacon

- *Business achievements* like an award for outstanding sales, getting a promotion, new job, new contract, or receiving a certification

- *Election to an office* in a political party, club, association, or professional society

Some Guidelines

WRITING IMMEDIATELY UPON LEARNING of someone's good news gives your note that clarion ring of sincerity. But if you've heard the news long after the fact, or if you have procrastinated, write anyway. Acknowledge that your greeting is late, but don't dwell on it.

Congratulations. I'm tardy with this note, but you certainly weren't with your timely op-ed piece in The Post. *It was an excellent and incisive evaluation.*

What a wonderful annual meeting! Congratulations on winning the election. I've now witnessed three of your efficiently run sessions, and I look forward to at least eight more with you at the gavel, Mr. President.

Congratulations on getting the Beckman contract! I just heard the news. It was a hard-won victory—I know because we bid it too—and I'm sure you'll do an excellent job.

Congratulations on an outstanding season, Series Champ! It's taken me a little while to write this note from here in the contenders' circle. You deserve the Cup for your excellent efforts.

Use these tips if you are having trouble getting started:

• Use the word "congratulations" early.

• State the occasion for congratulations in the first sentence or two.

• Start with an action verb that expresses your feelings, then put it into a sentence:

Congratulations, Jimmy, you won the day.

You drove in the winning run to clinch the series. What a champ.

Congratulations. You cut overhead by 37 percent in four months. What great news.

You pushed sales over the top, and it's a real pleasure to congratulate you on your promotion.

You sunk the winning shot! Congratulations!

• Write like you'd speak to the person, conversationally. (That goes for a friend as well as a business associate.)

. . . Alain, we've been friends for ten years, and I always admire your perseverance, but never more than I did . . .

Susan, I know how many hours of your personal time you gave up, and how many baseball games you missed to get this project off the ground. . . .

• Connect the person to the achievement, occasion, event, or happy news.

. . . Everyone knows your team wouldn't have won without your dedicated efforts. . . .

. . . Bob, your coaching is what produced the win today. . . .

. . . Nancy, congratulations on the new kitchen. I see your expert taste and practicality in every gleaming detail. . . .

• If it's appropriate, tell the person how you learned the news, include a newspaper clipping, or refer to a shared memory.

Allison, congratulations on making the quarterfinals. What a nice write-up in The Post, *page 5D today (enclosed). . . .*

Congratulations, Beverly! I saw you listed as a brand-new CPA in the alumni newsletter enclosed.

Congratulations. Mom tells me you finished the triathlon in second place in your age category.

• Relate something that bears on the occasion or event (but be sure to keep your message focused on the recipient).

All those cross-court forehand drills you practiced, practiced, practiced, until well after dark have paid off. . . .

You have shown outstanding discipline over these three years of study. . . .

I can hardly wait to hear all the details of your conditioning and training program. No one does it better. . . .

• Make sure your congratulations have a single focus: the person and her good news.

• End by expressing your best wishes for continued success.

I know your career is going all the way to the top. . . .

I'm sure you'll finish in first place next year.

We know we'll be voting for you, our favorite candidate, many times in the coming years.

• Your message needn't be long. Three to six sentences will do.

Reread your note—even aloud to yourself if you're uncertain—to be sure it has the ring of sincerity, and expresses what you want to say. I often write the note first in my spiral "drafts" notebook, then put it aside. When I pick it up again after an hour or two, I reread it to make sure I'm satisfied that it conveys what I want to say.

Louis,
    What a terrific job! Congratulations on winning the Suggestion of the Year Award. It was well deserved: your idea is brilliant, and I can hardly wait to see it implemented.
    You have a bright future at Rockethead.

Best regards,
Jorge

Dear Jose,
    Congratulations on becoming a citizen. It's wonderful news. Now you can test the rest of us on our history.
    We're proud to call you a fellow American.

Yours truly,
Arnie

Dear Aunt Ginger,

Congratulations on winning first place for your apple pie. Your family knew, of course, it has always been the very best, but now the whole county has proclaimed it.

You are a master in the kitchen.

Your devoted niece,
Tyler

6

Birthdays

Life began for me when you were born . . .
—RONALD REAGAN,
to wife Nancy

I WAS REMINDED RECENTLY just how important it is to send a special, personal birthday greeting when I was visiting an elderly aunt several weeks after her birthday. Still displayed predominantly across the sideboard in her dining room stood an array of a dozen bright and flowery birthday cards. I realized, as she retold the contents, she had obviously gone over each of the written messages many times. Her favorite, she said, was a blob of red construction paper, the attempt of a small child to shape a heart. Inside, in big, misshapen letters that ran to the edge of the paper and curved down to a tail of tiny letters, was penciled, *"Happy Birthday. I love you, Grammy. Asa."*

We're never too old or too young for a celebration of life. Birthdays are the ideal opportunity not only to celebrate someone's life, but also to add the glow of your special best wishes, and to nurture your relationship. There are only two secrets to making your greeting effective: make sure you write a personal message that is focused on the person you're writing to, and send it on time.

The timing part can be simple if you keep a current listing of friends' and family members' birth dates. I update my computer list and calendar each year. In fact, to promote melded and extended family relationships, last year I created a family calendar with all the special dates—including birthdays—noted. I then gave copies to family members as Christmas gifts. (My calendar included pictures of last year's birthday celebrations for the months in which the birthdays occur.)

Toward the end of each month, I take a look at the upcoming month's birthdays and select appropriate cards from my supply; or I put a special card purchase on my shopping list. I address each envelope early, and pencil a mailing date in the upper right-hand corner. Closer to mailing time, I write a special message inside, enclose a tiny gift or something of special interest, place a commemorative postage stamp over the penciled date, and mail the card so it will arrive in perfect time.

Sometimes I make birthday cards. I find it takes less time than shopping for commercial greeting cards, since I keep some basic supplies on hand. And it makes a very personal and special greeting for the person who appreciates such things. If you try it, I think you'll find that this lets you get the children involved, too, and helps you teach them how important—and how much fun—it is to care for others in this way. One especially meaningful kind of card for children to make for grandparents is easily done by using a blank card you may purchase that has a picture opening on the front. You just slip in a photograph and write your message inside.

Or, create your own photo card by folding a sheet of construction paper in half, and then in half again. Cut a rectangle or heart-shaped hole in the front, a bit smaller than the photo you'll insert, put several tiny spots of glue or rubber cement on the corners of the photograph, and center it beneath the opening you've created. It becomes a greeting from the entire family if everyone is in the photo. You may want the children to hold up a "Happy Birthday" sign, and wear birthday party hats. Some such cards I've received have been festooned with a generous sprinkling of glitter (which I *don't* recommend), or feature water-painted or crayoned "pictures" with wonderful, fledgling messages in original script. I always place these in a picture album or keepsake box.

Making your own card is not a just-for-kids thing. A simple handcrafted card from a college student to his mother was made from a piece of parchment to which dried flowers had been applied. The paper was folded lengthwise, and a tiny gold string was stretched into the fold and tied in a bow. The string held a separate inside sheet of parchment in place.

On it was this handwritten message:

Mom,

"In a mother's heart, we are always welcome."
—MARGARET BOYD.

I love you and hope that each year we continue to grow our friendship. You are the best. Happy B-Day.

Love,
Chris

If you add a handcrafted little gift, or a special purchase by a grandchild, all the better. Something like a homemade bookmark, croakie (cord to attach to glasses for around-the-neck wear), rubber jar lid gripper, potholder, key chain, or commemorative stamps (for the collector) will be cherished.

On birthday morning you can even crown the event and reinforce your message by telephoning the person of honor, and having everyone sing. Consider doing a "conference sing" with relatives in other locations. Or, you can send an e-mail birthday card, with a coordinated audio and animated message, as an added surprise. Now, won't Grandma be thrilled?

Who Is Having a Birthday?

FOCUSING ON THE BIRTHDAY person really starts with knowing how she feels about her day. Your greeting won't be meaningful—and could be irritating, or even offensive—if you don't do a little checking first.

Many women over thirty don't want their age mentioned, of course. If the birthday girl is feeling blue about turning forty, weigh this fact carefully before sending a greeting, and consider your alternatives. I have a friend who honestly didn't want the day acknowledged, period. So I didn't send a card. Instead, a few days before the date I wrote a note expressing how much I appreciate her. Here's part of what I wrote:

> *Dear Ardis,*
>
> *. . . I haven't ever told you this, but whenever you come to mind I think of perfect pitch. You've never seemed to hit a flat or false note in these ten years I've known you. And I've never known you to condemn or unduly criticize a single person, though any number of times I'd have done it in a New York nanosecond if I'd been wearing your shoes.*
>
> *. . . You're a wonderful person, and I'm so proud to call you "friend."*
>
> *Affectionately,*
> *Sandy*

Another friend pronounced herself "depressed" when she turned sixty-five because, she said, "Now I'm officially old. From here on out it's Social Security, false teeth, and everything starting to fall apart. I think old people are marginalized in our society, and that makes me very sad." Here's part of the message I sent:

Dear Ruth,

. . . I count your fresh ideas among the best, and your sparkling, new creativity and exuberance are special and unique. How fortunate and blessed I feel to have you for a friend. . . .

The Purchased Card

MOST OF US NOW depend on commercial greeting cards. I love receiving them, as long as they include a handwritten and personal message, too. The truth is that sometimes you find a card that so perfectly expresses what you cannot that it makes your heart soar.

But be sure—no matter how perfect the message—to include some of your own words. Here are some that were written below a wonderful printed message:

Sweetheart, This is from your tongue-tied Lover. I feel so fortunate to have found a card that so perfectly expresses my thoughts and feelings for you. So real, so heartfelt. I love you.

Your Buckets

You, too, can find exactly the right words to add to such a perfectly prewritten card. And don't hesitate to use quotes from songs, plays, poems, headlines, and even advertisements.

Is This a "Big Birthday"?

SOME BIRTHDAYS ARE BIGGER than others. Not only are the decade-marking birthdays large, but others are almost universally so: sixteen, because it signifies the huge step of being able to hold a driver's license. Eighteen usually means the legal drinking age, voting age, college age, and out-into-the-world-of-adulthood age. For some girls it is the official entry into society with debutante balls and coming-out parties. Turning twenty-one is another milestone, of course.

Many people report that turning thirty was monumental because it signaled that they were no longer trying on adulthood, but had solidly entered the grown-up phase of their lives—mistakes wouldn't be so easily forgiven, and decisions would take on more serious consequences. There is, for many, a realization: "Oh, so this is what I'm going to be when I grow up."

The reverse is infrequently true: I heard a young woman television news anchor say, "Whew, I was so happy to finally turn thirty. What a relief not to any longer hear all those 'kid' comments." For her, obviously, it meant gaining adult professional status.

Try to be sensitive about all these possibilities, and to how the birthday person feels. Whenever I can, I listen carefully to what the person says about an upcoming birthday, and take all of this into account when writing a birthday greeting.

A Matter of Sensitivities

"DON'T KID AROUND ABOUT being old," a friend told me after she opened a card from her sister-in-law that referred not too delicately to her age. Many sensitivities center on age, and it's important to know that it's not only mid-lifers who don't want their age published. Younger people can also be sensitive about telling when they began life on the planet. I was amazed to hear a man who was turning thirty-four, and still a college undergraduate, refer to himself as a "kid." By the same token, I was shocked to learn that a new relative was upset that she was turning thirty—so upset, in fact, she wouldn't discuss it. A woman turning thirty-two didn't want a candle placed in her cake at a celebration birthday luncheon; and a young man turning twenty-seven didn't want to have his age mentioned because, he said, he'd set a number of life goals for himself to reach by age twenty-five, and he felt he hadn't come close to accomplishing them. To everyone else's mind he'd accomplished a phenomenal amount; he was, in fact, an overachiever by most standards. These examples demonstrate why the general rule for adults is not to mention age at all.

On one of Nancy Reagan's White House birthdays, Ronald Reagan wrote on the envelope of her card: "*1st Lady, 1st Sweetheart, 1st Wife.*" The cover of the card was a big, graphic "29." Inside, the message he printed:

> *Just a reminder that our wonderful birthday season with its holiday spirit has come to an end—But you are still 29 to me no matter what this smart alec card says.*
> [Card text] *Isn't that carrying recession a little too far? Happy Birthday!*
>
> > *I love you*
> > *Your Pres*

Children are another matter. They are nearly always eager to be another year older, and mentioning this fact, along with all the things it means the child will be able to do in the coming year, is a great way to start the celebration.

Light Messages

FOR MEN WHO HAVE athletic interests, reference to their sport of choice is usually safe territory. It works especially well for the man you know primarily as an athlete but don't otherwise know well. Here are a few themes that are good starters:

For the champ who saved our socks in more than one softball tournament, here's to another winning season. I'm sure you'll out-perform last year on and off the field, and in everything you do. All my best wishes for a home run year!

Best wishes for a wonderful new year, and another ice-dancing trophy. Your skating, like good wine, just keeps getting better. You skate like the wind, Mike. Will this make six trophies when you win this year?

Seven years old! Does that mean you'll really be playing soccer this year? Wait till the Cardinals hear about this!

A little bird told me you're six years old today. Oh, I can just imagine all the exciting things you'll be able to do now: first grade, T-ball, and tennis lessons. I'm looking forward to your summer visit when you and I can play tennis together. I love you. How wonderful that you're six.

Ten years old! Now that you've entered double digits there's just no stopping you. Your dad tells me this means you'll have two new responsibilities, and two new privileges. How exciting. I can hardly wait to hear what these will be, and everything about them. I love you, and I know you are going to make a wonderful ten-year-old, since you were so great at nine!

You certainly distinguished yourself last year with two promotions and a brand-new home. I can't imagine what great things you have planned for this year. That windsurfing course, and new tennis gear? Here's a sweatband I got for you at Wimbledon to help launch your Grand Slam start, Ace! Happy birthday, and our best wishes for another Number One year.

After being named "Volunteer of the Year" last year, what do you plan for an encore? I can hardly wait to see; you simply amaze me. Whatever you decide, you'll add your unique Midas touch.

I'm so glad to hear you'll be running track this year. You're going to do exceptionally well, given your outstanding "Barker" athletic ability.

We feel so blessed to have you as a son-in-law. We couldn't have designed a better one, given the whole realm of possibilities. We want to wish you a day of joy, and a year filled with great ski, golf, and Big Brother fun.

The world may know you as Chris Mobley, but in our hearts you're simply Mr. Perfectly Wonderful! We couldn't have ordered a better nephew. Happy birthday, Champ.

Seriously, Who Are You?

WHILE YOU'RE THINKING about the person, try focusing on her more serious qualities that you most admire, and let them direct your pen. Has she shown strength in difficult times; is she a wonderful parent; is she an accomplished negotiator; does she have a talent for singing she's particularly proud of; is she a wonderful daughter-in-law; a great chef; a skilled organizer; energetic; resourceful; calm in the face of turbulence; humorous; always optimistic; or very spiritual? Use any of these attributes as a good place to start your note of celebration. Consider, too, of course, what her attributes have meant to you and how they have impacted others:

> *Dear Jenny,*
>
> *I'll never forget the day of the fire, and how—when everyone else was exhibiting stage-three hysteria—you quietly loaded up everything in five minutes, then organized and helped evacuate seven neighborhood families in another forty.*
>
> *You bring calm to chaos. And you've brought serenity and real and solid joy to my life, and to Philip's. It's a wonderful thing to experience, and a beautiful thing to see. I'm so happy to have the opportunity to celebrate your life.*
>
> *Thank you for all you do, and have a happy, happy birthday.*
> *Yours affectionately*
> *Rachel*

> *Dear Sarah,*
>
> *You are one of a very elite group: teachers who have made a real, life-changing and lifelong difference in your students' lives. I know you did in mine.*

Thank you for being you, thank you for being there, and thank you for being my teacher. I will never forget your wonderful lessons in life.

Happy birthday.

Love,
Ted

Nurturing Relationships

OFTEN THE KEY TO the perfect message comes from identifying the roots of your relationship with the person, and making a plan to continue to build on it. Some relationships are rooted in a common history, some in common blood, and some on common circumstances, interests, or personality traits. Focusing on these commonalities can help you express something especially meaningful.

Building a continuing and caring relationship over time, of course, takes some effort. But it needn't be expensive; it can just be time spent together. You can provide for this in your special greeting by adding a line and making a plan to do something to celebrate her birthday together:

. . . I propose a birthday toast on Friday, High Tea at Gilfords, 4:00 P.M. Will that work for you?

. . . Remember when we were sixteen and our favorite thing was to steal away for a Saturday afternoon of shopping? We're overdue! Let's do a Frannie, very special (non-Prom) birthday shopping afternoon at Irongate on Saturday. I suggest meeting in Nordstrom's shoe department at 1:00 P.M. That will get us started off on the right foot!

. . . *Let's sit together at the junior high basketball game on Friday. I'm so eager to hear all about your trip.*

. . . *Let's meet at Mom's on June 7. Sisters shouldn't be strangers, and sisters' birthdays should be celebrated by sisters together. I love you, Sis, and I miss you.*

. . . *E-mail doesn't quite do it for birthdays. I miss your superb company. How about a birthday drink after work Thursday, say 5:15 P.M., at Barney's?*

. . . *A day at the zoo! A day at the zoo! That's what I think would be really fun to do! How about you? Let's do a Zack and Grandma birthday day at the zoo!*

. . . *How about doing Jessie's special birthday lunch with Grandma on Saturday? We can top it off with a candle in the mud pie!*

Birthday Notes to Your Child

IF YOU'RE A PARENT, you'll want to remember to send a very special card to each of your children. These will be the stuff of many happy times of reflection as they grow older. Be sure to include all the unique things they do, their favorite words and phrases, what they look like, who their special friends are, their favorite foods and activities, and so forth. Include every detail that will later paint a true picture of who they were at this age, and save your card in an album or keepsake box.

Gracie,

Two years old today, and you are our precious and perfect angel—in fact, that's what your Grandma Stokes calls you, "Angel Cakes." Daddy calls you "My Pookie Pie," and I call you "Sweet Gracie." We're each thoroughly convinced that our special name is just right!

You are a real conversationalist for just two years old, spouting phrases like, "Mother, today I must wear my red dress." You have, in fact, been talking in complete sentences for nearly the whole year. When I ask you why the red dress, you place your chubby hands on those round little hips and respond with an exaggerated sigh, "Well, it's Tuesday, and that's red dress day." We have no idea how you arrived at this explanation, unless it was because you overheard Aunt Emma say she was wearing her jeans to work on casual Friday: "Casual Friday is jean day."

The doctor says you're in the ninety-five percentile for height and weight for your age, and your family is all certain that means you'll be tall and willowy like the Wright side of your genetic pool. Of course the Stokes believe you'll be gifted in math, and have perfect pitch. Grandma Stokes has even tried to test you already, hitting a note on the piano, then telling you to sing it. You're making her beam and declare, "Gracie possesses exceptional musical talent." One of your favorite activities is going to her house, getting Miss Sniff, the Persian cat, up on the piano bench between you and Grandma, and singing "Down on the Farm" with her. You know all the words, and can even sing the melody while Grandma harmonizes. She's planning to have you two do a duet for her bridge club next month.

We're all sure that your head of golden curls will remain a lifelong crowning glory, and you'll be a talented swimmer and triathlete like Grandma Wright.

Of course, my dear one, all this burden of expectations comes to you because you were so long awaited, and all of our love buckets were overflowing before you ever got here. We love you so!

Your favorite friend this year is four-year-old Beatrice, who moved in across the street, and you two have a play morning once every other week. Yesterday you had a tea party with your dolls: Mrs. Fritz and Baby Alice. We served cucumber sandwiches and molasses cookies—your favorites.

This year you've discovered hamburgers and french fries, much to the horror of Aunt Emma, who firmly believes fast foods should be totally shunned, and we should be sent to parenting school for ever allowing you to taste either.

Today we're also having your favorite cake, carrot, with butter and cream cheese frosting, and two huge candles. Helium balloons are everywhere. You love them, and so does Snoopy, the wire-haired terrier. The two of you have devised a game of seek-and-destroy: you grasp a string and pull a balloon down, and she jumps up, grabs it, and attacks it until she gets it to pop. We'll all laugh at this video our entire lives.

Your favorite gift at our little family party was the Chinese blue tea set in the photograph. We've already scheduled another tea party with Beatrice for Friday afternoon.

With all our love,
Mommy and Daddy

Messages to Cheer and Encourage

IT'S NEVER A BAD idea to point out the best part of turning the corner into a new year, as long as your statements don't ring with preachy overtones or the buzz of patronization. Sometimes your own experience can be cheering, even inspirational:

Dear Clemmie,

When I turned fifty—not that long ago; okay, a while ago—I was preoccupied with what I hadn't accomplished. How silly I feel now. Everything was still so possible. My life, I now see, had all kinds of potential. In fact, as you know, I built my entire company after I turned fifty-five. (But enough about me.)

I realize you're just a kid in the total scope of things. I've always admired your shoot-for-the-moon attitude and abilities. You've got the real stuff*, Clemmie, and I'm sure you're going to launch one of those stellar efforts I've seen you mastermind and execute so proficiently, and so often. Like getting up in college in front of five hundred people, without a minute of preparation or practice, and delivering the winning temperance speech! (I'll never forget your speech, or your chutzpa.) You are truly phenomenal!*

Next year at this time, I'll be back here again, saluting what you've done since your new year began. Of that I'm very sure.

Happy Birthday, Girl Friend. All the very best!

Love,
Bonnie

A Year of Loss

SOMETIMES BIRTHDAYS ARE BITTERSWEET. If the birthday person is facing her first year without her husband, or has recently lost her mother, a child, a sibling, or a beloved pet, it's best not to ignore the loss. It's also important to know how (even if) she wishes to have others refer to it. If you're not sure, try to find out. Even ask. Often it's best to simply make a brief mention of it, then focus on the person you're writing to.

Dear Cece,

    I realize celebrating your birthday without Rafe is going to be difficult, but he'd be the first to tell you, "Life is a celebration. Grasp it with both hands." Just like you've always done. Just like you always will. In that spirit, and because of the wonderful person you are, I'd love to take you to lunch at our favorite place, Saddie's, on Saturday. I suggest picking you up at 11:30 A.M.

Love,
Eleanor

Dear Sally,

    I remember so well when Grace, you, and I had your special twelfth birthday party. Even though she can't be with us this year in body, I know she is in spirit, and I'd like to suggest we get together and celebrate your birthday, just like she did with us for the past twenty years. Let's even have it at your favorite place, the Wellshire. Can you make it Friday for lunch?

Yours always,
Alice

Start a Tradition

FOR SPECIAL FRIENDS AND close relatives you may want to create a birthday tradition, like building a memory box or birthday album for a friend, sister, daughter, niece, or granddaughter. You could chose to have her participate and contribute something special about her hopes for the year, and something special from the previous year. Or you could keep it a secret, and make your own contribution with the plan to give her the box or album as a gift when she turns twenty-one. Or forty.

    Another tradition could be meeting at a special place, or doing something like going out for a birthday hot fudge sundae, or attending a baseball game. Birthday parties can also be a tradition, as simple as a bouquet of balloons, dinner, silly hats, and the same special birthday cake. An album of all these parties would become a treasure trove of memories if presented to the birthday person after a decade or more.

Business Birthdays

IN DECIDING WHETHER AND how to celebrate birthdays for colleagues, it's usually best to consider office policy. Then consider the repercussions of sending a birthday card to a subordinate, for example. This could mean that you should also send a greeting to two hundred subordinates. The best approach is usually a card from the entire department or group with signatures and brief notes. Some departments make it a practice to have a birthday cake during coffee break, or an after-work drink. Some have a special coffee break cake once a month and announce all the birthdays.

Envelope Gifts

THERE'S A LONG AND lovely list of gifts (inexpensive to costly) that can be easily tucked into an envelope to make your greeting even more memorable. Of course, you can also tuck your card into a package with just the right gift. If a child makes a bookmark, it will undoubtedly become a cherished talisman to a grandmother or grandfather. "Love Coupons" are my favorite. They represent something very special to come, to anticipate, or promised contact with a person.

Coupons work well because they can be tailored to the age, personality, and preferences of the birthday person. I've used everything from "Good for one apple pie upon twenty-four-hour notice," for my husband (along with a whole booklet of treats he especially enjoys), to "Good for one summer afternoon at Miss Piggy's Costume Tea Party" for a five-year-old. (At the last such event an adult invitee came in the summer heat to our outdoor party, dressed in her best stole, wearing white gloves, and bearing a bouquet of fresh gladioli.) Ideas for these coupons are limitless. The trick is knowing the person you're gifting.

A Laughing Matter

HUMOR ISN'T FOR EVERYONE. Many of my elderly friends don't care to receive humorous cards. So make sure your sense of humor, and that of your greeting, is shared by the birthday person. Just because something makes you laugh, it isn't a forgone conclusion that she will think it's funny. When in doubt, don't. I've seen greetings go seriously wrong when they contained a barb, or poked fun at the birthday person. Today isn't the day she wants to think about being older than Roy Rogers' horse, or in need of a diet or antiaging creams. Blonde jokes and clichés won't reflect how special you think she is, either.

The Belated Greeting

NO ONE FEELS GOOD about being delinquent in sending a birthday greeting, especially to a close friend or relative, but for any number of reasons the day can slip off the best of radar screens. If it happens, be honest, briefly state that you regret missing the date, and send your recipient-centered greeting. It's never too late for you to join the celebration. Here are a few ideas:

   . . . *This is the earliest I've ever been late!*

. . . *Remember when Greg Dever told the third grade teacher that the dog really did eat his assignment? Well, I'm not going to tell you that one, but would you believe that the cat flipped it behind the desk, and that's where I found it this morning?*

. . . *Late, but still every word is true and comes from my heart with my best wishes.*

. . . *I'm suffering from calendar failure: I forgot to note that your birthday comes on the very first day of the month. I must learn to preview. I hope your day was wonderful, and all the good wishes come true.*

. . . *Whose Grandma got stuck in Atlanta and didn't get Troy's card and gift mailed? I think this calls for a Grandma penalty. How about one chocolate malted milk served up at Jake's after Little League Monday?*

. . . *You'd think that since you're so often in my thoughts, it would be impossible for me to let the day slip by without sending this birthday wish. But then you'd realize that my Palm Pilot doesn't remind me unless I turn it on. Oy! I promise to do better next year.*

. . . *It's an imperfect world, and I'm an imperfect birthday greeting sender. I have no excuse. The wishes are for a nearly perfect person, however. And every word is true, true, true.*

. . . *On time? No. Sincere and heartfelt? Yes. Yes. Yes.*

About the Little Ones

THIS IS THE BIGGEST event in a small child's life, so make it very special. If you can't be there, send the card a few days early for the thrill of anticipation.

You might even decide to send a series of little greetings leading up to the big day, sending one a week that has a puzzle or clues on it:

Hmmm . . . I was just wondering whose birthday is coming up. Can you tell me?

How many days?

Who wants to play "Pin the Tail on the Donkey" on his birthday?

It's important, too, to keep all your greetings in synch with the age of the child. If in doubt, check with another child or two the same age. A clown card sent to a ten-year-old girl might not send the right message.

Make a party in the envelope by including a dollar for each year the child is old, or for a small child use coins to festoon the card. Include a special balloon with "Happy Birthday" written on it to blow up, or buy an activity like punch-out, put-togethers made for envelope mailing. A few more ideas for a child's envelope: special shoe laces that stay tied; hair barrettes, bands, and ribbons; plastic store "credit cards" for a favorite clothing or book store; gift certificates; an audio or video disc; a tiny book; baseball, basketball, hockey, or other sports cards for collecting; commemorative postage stamps for collecting; and special card games like "Authors," or "Fish." Coupons, created by you, or gift certificates to ice cream shops or kids' toy stores are always welcome.

7

Graduations

The heights by great men reached and kept
Were not attained by sudden flight,
But they, while their companions slept,
Were toiling upward in the night.
—HENRY WADSWORTH LONGFELLOW;
"The Ladder of Saint Augustine"

THERE ARE FEW TIMES in life more delightful than celebrating a graduation. It ranks right up there behind births and weddings, neatly signaling a triumphant end and a fresh new beginning. As a society, we love it so much, in fact, that we've extended the concept of "graduating" to include graduating from preschool, kindergarten, grade school, and junior high school, as well as high school, college, and graduate studies. Graduation never loses its luster, though, and each event gives us another opportunity to connect with a brand new graduate.

Not every student is a star, of course, and I've known graduates—and their parents—for whom the ceremony was more of a relief than a celebration. Still, this is an important milestone, and whatever the scholastic record, or however narrow the margin of success, you can emphasize some positive elements of a graduate's achievement.

I find that tapping into my own experiences of graduating is a great place to start when drafting a note. What do I remember?

What was I feeling? Yes, relief does come to mind. So does anticipation, achievement, setting new goals, apprehension, reflecting on values, and taking a look at my whole life and evaluating my progress.

Tuning in to the graduate is a second key: how does *she* feel about this event? Being a "high achiever" and a star in high school doesn't necessarily mean your niece or nephew is confident about starting college. (It also doesn't mean she or he even plans to go to college.) So, be sure you're tuned in, or keep your note general:

Susie, Congratulations on finishing the course. That, in itself, is a grand achievement. . . .

Derek, A wonderful thing about where you are—high school graduation—is looking back and seeing how far you've come. . . .

April, What a great day it is. You now have that diploma in your hand. . . .

I then try to mention whatever highlights I've learned about the graduate's achievements. If she was a cheerleader, captain of the debate team, class president, basketball star, honor student, or biology major, I usually include that information.

. . . I admire your skill and ability to rise like a butterfly and execute those dunks on the basketball court. What a long way you've come from the third grader who used to get called for standing in the paint. . . .

. . . As class president you've demonstrated the kind of leadership that will allow you to excel in everything you do in life. . . .

. . . Having been captain of the debate team will help you in so many ways. . . .

. . . Wow, on the honor roll and an all-star athlete! This family has never had such an overachiever, and we are overjoyed. . . .

Whatever the graduate's record, you can find something to praise. A friend's son refused his parents' pleas to apply himself to his academic studies; he was only interested in his music classes and creating a rock band. To this graduating musician I wrote:

Lewis, You have both a huge talent for music, and a talent for knowing exactly what you want. It's a great combination for getting you where you want to go. We know you will do very well in the Bruster Program. . . .

Another friend's daughter found high school extremely difficult, but she was determined to finish. To her I began:

Rosie, You've demonstrated the very best qualities in life: The ability to face a difficult challenge, to set your goal, and then to see it through to completion. Congratulations, high school graduate. You have done a fine job, and we are so excited about getting to see you walk across that stage and accept your diploma. . . .

Acknowledge any bittersweet aspect of her achievement, or some difficulty she has overcome. For a young graduating friend whose father was transferred just as her senior year began, I wrote:

Jennifer, Congratulations. The kids who did it the easy way may not appreciate how brave you've been. But we do! You've exhib-

ited real character, maturity, and determination moving to a new school, making up class requirements, and still graduating on time. You're a very special person, and have demonstrated that you have what it takes to succeed at anything you decide to do. . . .

You may make the experience sweeter for the graduate by noting how she has matured:

It's been a long and beautiful process you've completed, and we've been so thrilled to watch you develop into the outstanding young woman you've become.

Your third-grade interest in collecting bugs, it seems, is leading to a fascinating career in biology.

It's a wonderful thing to see that the little girl who used to beat me at "horse" out at the garage basketball hoop is going to become a college hoops star at State . . .

Let your message look to the future, and express optimism about the graduate's prospects:

We know you've set your sights on becoming a doctor, and we have every confidence you'll achieve that, too.

The most wonderful thing about this whole graduation thing is seeing what a mature young lady that little tomboy has become. And you've become an outstanding scholar, too.

This is a prime time for some inspiring words, and passing on a bit of wisdom, especially if you have known the graduate well and long, or have been her respected teacher or mentor. Particularly poignant quotes or verses can be very effective:

Albert Camus said, "Any authentic creation is a gift to the future."

"Try again. Fail again. Fail better."—Samuel Beckett.

"Oh, the places you'll go now!" Dr. Seuss said.

"A book should be as an axe, to break the frozen sea within us," said Franz Kafka.

"Poets are the unacknowledged legislators of the world."—Percy Bysshe Shelley.

"O! for a Muse of fire, that would ascend The brightest heaven of invention," William Shakespeare wrote.

"Writing does not exclude the full life. It demands it."—Katherine Anne Porter.

"Treat every moment with reverence."—Bharati Mukherjee.

8

Engagements

There's nothing half so sweet in life
As love's young dream.
—THOMAS MOORE

ONE OF LIFE'S MOST JOYOUS EVENTS is the announcement of a couple's engagement. Although time-worn traditions, lifestyles, formalities, and mores have all dramatically changed in the last few decades, many of these changes have created an even greater emphasis on the moment when two people become engaged, a statement that says, "We're committed to share our lives with each other." It's a wonderful time to embrace the couple in a declaration of their new unity. And it's a great time to share in, and enlarge, their joy.

The Announcement

AFTER THE IMMEDIATE FAMILY members have been told the happy news, a broader announcement may be made by handwritten notes or letters to other family members and friends, and by placing an announcement in newspapers and other publications.

Dear Cherri,
  I have great news! I'm getting married . . .

You, the bride- (or groom-)to-be, will probably then want to follow up with some details. You'll undoubtedly want to include the name of your future partner, and a little bit about him, and the date you plan to marry, if you've decided.

But you'll probably also want to add things like how the two of you met, how long you've known each other, how happy you are, and how eager you are for the recipient to meet your intended.

. . . My fiance's name is Patterson Whipple. He's British, and I met him two years ago in my law firm, Lawton and Boughers, where he's a managing partner. We do, of course, have career goals in common, and so much more. (I'll tell all when we get together next month.) I can hardly wait for you to meet him. You, of all people, will appreciate his wry sense of humor. I'm sure you'll get on famously, and Jack will want to book regular dates with "Pat," since he, too, is a 5.5 level tennis player. Doubles, anyone?

. . . Remember those long, dreamy conversations we two pubescents used to have about the men we'd marry? (Soon we both will have!) Pat surpasses all those girlish daydreams, except he's taller and even more handsome. Really. He's perfect, and we're so happy! . . .

If you have placed the announcement in the newspaper, you might include a copy of this, too.

If you are having an engagement party, this note may also be an invitation to that event.

. . . Mom and Dad are busy choreographing an engagement party scheduled for January 15 at the club, so please save the date

*(official invitation to follow). I don't want to steal Mom's thun-
der here. She's ecstatic that her hopelessly single daughter may yet
get married; and perhaps may still produce some grandchildren!*

Love,
Crystal

Congratulations

JOIN IN THE CELEBRATION by writing a response of congratulations that focuses on the couple and your wish for their happiness
together. A friend wrote this note to the new prospective groom in
response to the news:

Daryl,

*If my calculations are correct, we've been "buds" for twenty
years now. Wow! (I remember the day you selected me to be on
your basketball team. A proud moment in my childhood.) I won't
review what we've been through together, but we both know we've
seen each other at some of our most zenith, as well as nadir,
moments, and still remain best friends. So, when I say that I never
thought there was another person on the planet like you, it comes
with some knowledge and conviction. That was true until I met
Carmen. After that meeting, I said to Joanna, "I can't believe it,
but I've just met Daryl's counterpoint. She's perfect for him."*

*So, I wasn't surprised at your wonderful news. And I couldn't
be more delighted for you. I believe you two will remain soul
mates and best of friends for a lifetime. (This doesn't, of course,
mean you'll get a pass on our Thursday evening basketball games.)
Congratulations!*

Your best bud,
David

Try to write soon after receiving the news, to underscore your enthusiasm and sincerity. You may want to address your congratulations to the couple together, if you know them both; and you may also want to send a note to the mother and/or father, even to a sibling of the bride or groom, if you know one well. Your notes will go far to help form the kind of community of relatives and friends that can begin to welcome and embrace a couple in a blanket of love and caring.

No longer do you have to worry about the exact words to use in your greeting. While once upon a time it was proper to use "congratulations" in your note to a future groom, and "best wishes" to a future bride, it's now perfectly acceptable to use these words interchangeably.

If you have reservations about the match, keep them to yourself; but don't manufacture a false enthusiasm. If your concerns are major, they should be dealt with personally and privately in conversation—and never in writing. But remember that it's much more important to keep your relationship with the intended partners intact, than it is to express doubts and fracture your bonds. Where the heart is concerned, objectivity is usually absent or in very short supply. You will most likely alienate a friend or relative by expressing your concerns. If asked by the betrothed for your endorsement or opinion, look for a positive and supportive way to express your concern for the person's happiness:

> *Julian, Only you can make the choice of a mate. I trust your judgment . . .*

> *Avery, I've known you since first grade, and I know you wouldn't make such an important decision without being very sure . . .*

Focus the note on your love for the person you're writing to, and the joy he or she has expressed; truly and sincerely extend your wishes for his or her happiness, and for the life of the couple together. Here are some examples:

Dear Dana,

Your mom has just written that you and Pearson Staples are to be married. She says you're walking on clouds, and she doesn't think you'll come down for years. That's the best news I've had since I received word that I had a brand new niece, and her name was to be Dana.

I'm thrilled for you, my dearest one, and I look forward to performing any wedding assignment you may wish to give me.

Your happiness matters a great deal to Uncle Jerry and me, and we can hardly wait to meet Pearson. We know that if you love him, we will too. May we host a small engagement party for you and invite your friends still here in Dallas?

Lovingly,
Aunt Rose

Dear Erika and Elizah,

Joy, joy, joy! That's what's been ringing in my heart since I got your call this morning. I'm so happy for you. It is evident that you two are a perfect match, and deeply in love. I look forward to embracing you two as a couple, and wish you every happiness.

Overjoyed,
Jennifer

Dear Alicia,

It seems like only last week that you were the sweet and smiling girl next door who was always in the middle of a science project, and needed to borrow a jar, a cup of leaves, or some of that special compost Riley had then (for your worms).

Now, so soon, you're a bright and rising scientist and newly minted bride-to-be. Riley and I are overjoyed at your news, and look forward to meeting this "wonderful" man. We wish you happiness beyond measure.

Warmest wishes,
Georgia

Dear Rick (Formerly known as the Teflon Bachelor),
Of course we're sorry to lose you from our band of tried, confirmed, and merry single men, but we all know how much you and Jenny are meant for each other. So, we'll regretfully ring you out of the corps, and we'll try our best to celebrate your new status.
Love like yours is something very rare indeed, and I extend every good wish for your happiness together.

Best wishes
Rob

Introduction of the Families of the Bride and Groom

ALTHOUGH INTRODUCTIONS ARE NOW possible in an electronic nanosecond, a personal note is a welcome and lasting way to let these people with whom you will be connected know of your pleasure at the upcoming union, and to make a warm and cordial gesture of welcome. Traditionally, the parents of the groom call the bride's family to introduce themselves, express their delight, and arrange a meeting. Often the two families meet for a dinner and introductions, in which case invitations and thank yous can be expanded to express your wish for a future congenial relationship:

Dear Rebecca and Randolph,

To follow up on our telephone introductions, I'd just like to say, again, how happy Mark and I are at the news that Beth and Noah have become engaged. We have so enjoyed getting to know Beth over the past eight months, and realize we have a great advantage in this department, since they both live and work within thirty miles of us.

It will be a pleasure to meet the two people responsible for nurturing and guiding Beth in developing into the lovely young woman she has become. She is exceptionally mature, industrious, and delightful in every way.

I've enclosed a map to our house from the airport. We are eagerly looking forward to dinner on May 15th.

Sincerely and affectionately
Mark and Alice

Broken Engagements

IF AN ENGAGEMENT is broken after a formal announcement has been made, or even if the word has simply been informally announced, it is often easier and less painful to write a brief personal note to family and friends to inform them. I received one that stated, "I'm sorry to report that Stuart and I have decided not to marry." Another said simply, "I'm saddened to tell you that Rick and I won't be getting married on August 10 as planned. We have cancelled our engagement."

Certainly no elaborate details are required, and there is no need to give an explanation. (See chapter 9, Weddings.)

9

Weddings

Come live with me and be my love,
And we will all the pleasures prove
That valleys, groves, hills, and fields.
Woods or steepy mountain yields . . .
—CHRISTOPHER MARLOWE,
"The Passionate Shepherd to His Love"

DESPITE ALL THE CULTURAL CHANGES we've seen in the past few decades, marriage still remains one of the most sacred and meaningful relationships of our lives, and the joining together of the community around the couple adds depth and meaning.

Most of us still view marriage as the union of two people in a lifelong commitment to live and share their lives as one. Beyond this, the blessing of this contract creates a bond of unity among family members and friends. When you enter into this ceremony—at your own wedding or someone else's—it is truly a life-affirming event. (See chapter 8, Engagements.)

I recently attended two weddings where the officiating minister turned to the audience right after the couple exchanged their vows and said something like: "And to the family and friends gathered here, do you commit to support, encourage, embrace, comfort, and nourish this couple in their life together? Do you commit to hold them up, to comfort and succor them? If so, say 'I do.'"

This seems to me a wonderful and important thing, and something that can help create a community of support for the newly married couple.

There will be many opportunities to express your good wishes in writing, offer help, participate, and receive and give thanks to others involved. Join in with a full heart.

Because the wedding ceremony is tied to the couple's belief systems, your wishes for growth and happiness should be in tune with them. Whatever the beliefs, here are some of the commonly used, personal written expressions that should be part of the wedding events.

Notes from the Wedding Couple

- Informing close family and friends of the upcoming wedding
- Notifying an ex-spouse, if appropriate
- Announcements: newspaper, and printed formal or handwritten informal
- Introduction of the families of the bride and groom
- Wedding attendant and participant invitations
- Save-the-Date cards
- Guest invitations
- Postponement or cancellation
- Wedding rehearsal invitations
- Thank-you note cards for gifts

Wedding communications may be either traditional or unique. A couple who eloped sent a small, handwritten fold-over note card stating they had been married in a civil ceremony at the county courthouse. They invited me to a simple, small "gathering" of a few friends in their tiny new apartment. Conversely, I received a very formal invitation to a wedding halfway around the world, a fairytale orchestration of a high mass ceremony in a thirteenth-century cathedral, followed by a reception held in a castle's grand hall.

Here's a save-the-date preinvitation request:

> *To Our Dearest Family and Friends,*
>
> *Yes, dear ones, we are finally getting married. Our happy day will be September 8, and it is with full and hopeful hearts that we'd like to ask you to save the day to be present with us and help us make our public declaration of love and commitment complete by your presence.*
>
> *A formal invitation and all the details will follow.*
>
> *Warm personal regards,*
> *Sarah and Ben*

The Wedding Party Notes

WHILE THE HONOR OF BEING asked to serve as part of the wedding party is usually done in person or on the telephone, it is very nice to follow this up with written notes of invitation, confirmation, and acceptance. Be sure to include some of the reasons you asked this person to participate; and for acceptance, express your joy in being so honored. Be sure, too, that all of the basic information is laid out. You, the bride, should include an explanation of what the duties will entail, which should include a frank discussion of the costs. (Obviously, there may be a number of lengthy verbal discussions, too.) It's very important to consider this carefully, of course, because such an invitation usually means a substantial expense for the invitee, and acknowledging this, and allowing for a graceful way for her to decline, is necessary.

Dear Brett,

I know we agreed as kids that we would be in each others' weddings, and no one else can really fill your sisterly role as my maiden of honor. But I also know that your college expenses have been extremely high, and have caused a huge strain on your finances.

I also realize May 15 is undoubtedly finals time for you, but we couldn't set any other date because of Jared's overseas assignment.

I won't hold you to your promise, Sis. I'll completely understand if you must decline. If you must, I propose a first anniversary dinner together. Jared and I could come to San Franciso, and we could make it a very special occasion. What do you think?

Sisters forever,
Laura

Dear Jasmine,

Of course I'll be honored to be a bridesmaid at your wedding. What joy! I'll wait for your note with all the details, then I'll be in touch. What a happy day June 18 will be.

Best wishes always,
Paula

Dear Chelsea,

I'm so delighted you'll be my matron of honor. I really can't imagine walking down the aisle and not seeing you ahead of me, as you have been all my life, Big Sister. You've made my joy complete with your acceptance!

Your little sis,
Melody

Notifying an Ex-Spouse

THE NATURE AND FORM of this communication will depend on the character of your relationship, but there may also be legal reasons that make it necessary. Where much acrimony exists and no children are involved, the communication may actually be best made immediately after the ceremony.

> *Dear Isaiah,*
>
> *I wanted to let you know that on Saturday I married Jeremy Stone. I will now be legally Stephanie Stone, and will reside at 345 Adams, Berkeley, CA. Please send any communications to this address.*
>
> *Stephanie*

If your ex-spouse is the parent of your children, there are other reasons to communicate your news in as civil and amicable a manner as possible. While children should be told by the remarrying parent, there are many reasons to have the cooperation of your ex-spouse.

> *Dear Tina,*
>
> *I want you to hear this first and directly from me: Ingrid and I have decided to marry. I know you may have concerns about how this will affect the children, shared custody arrangements, and schedules, so I'd like for the three of us to sit down and try to amicably work this out in the best possible manner for the kids. We'd suggest a Saturday meeting in two weeks at Friskies. Say 10:30 A.M. Will that work for you?*
>
> *We haven't made any public announcement, and haven't told*

the children yet, since we felt the three of us needed to work out some of the basic details first.

Although our differences are many at this point, and our relationship is long fractured, we share a huge interest in the welfare of three little people, and I believe for their sakes we can commit to put aside all our personal conflicts and structure the best future possible for them.

Please let Ingrid and me know if you will be able to meet as suggested. If not, please suggest a workable time and place.

Sincerely,
Adam

Informal Wedding Invitation

WHILE MANY BOOKS HAVE been dedicated to the form and appearance of formal wedding invitations, inserts, RSVPs, regrets, and so forth, you may, for a small, informal wedding, wish to create a simple, informal invitation. In addition to making sure the information given is complete, maybe you'd like to begin your invitation with a warmer, more informal phrase:

. . . Theodora Trip and Brendon White invite you to celebrate their marriage . . .

. . . Joy Renate and James Dean would be honored to have you share the joy of the marriage of their daughter . . .

. . . Our joy will be complete if you will share in the marriage of our daughter . . .

. . . Alicia Stern and Alex Boughman invite you to their wedding . . .

. . . Our daughter, Judith Rae, will be married to Gunnar Hoarst, on Saturday . . . They will speak their vows at . . . We invite you to join us to witness their vows, and be our guest at a reception which follows . . .

Postponement or Cancellation

NO EXPLANATION NEED BE given if you decide to either postpone or cancel your wedding. You may simply write:

Dear Pam,

I'm so sorry to have to tell you that Richard and I have broken our engagement. I am, therefore, returning the lovely linen tablecloth and napkins you were so thoughtful to send us.

Love,
Eleanor

Or, you may more formally announce:

Mr. and Mrs. Justin Overton announce that the marriage of their daughter, Rachel, to Stephen Wells, will not take place.

Wedding Rehearsal Invitations

TRADITIONALLY, THE GROOM'S FAMILY hosts a dinner after the wedding rehearsal for participants. The minister and spouse usually attend, too, as do a few other select relatives and perhaps close friends.

The invitations are usually handwritten notes. I received one that simply asked that I save the time, and that details would be given at the rehearsal. A closing statement reassured me the dinner would end by early evening since the wedding was the following morning. I've also received formal invitations that laid out elaborate details, down to the fine points, and made the dinner part of an event. In either case, you will undoubtedly want the invitees to RSVP so you know how many will attend.

> *Dear Janet and Jack,*
>   *We are hosting a rehearsal dinner for Jennifer and Rafe, July 7, at 7:00 P.M., at Long Putts Country Club. Please join us. We look forward to hearing that you will be able to make it.*
>   *Warm personal regards,*
>   *Deanna (and David)*

Thank-You Notes for Gifts and Good Wishes

SENDING THANK-YOU NOTES gives the new couple another opportunity to connect with each of the well-wishers. Use notes created from the same paper as your wedding invitations, and send them no later than three months after the wedding. If gifts arrive before the wedding, thank-you notes may be written as gifts are received. Also send a personal note to each person who has sent a telegram or other forms of special good wishes. While these notes used to be written by the bride and addressed to the wife of the gift-giving couple, today this task is often equally shared by the newly (or not-yet) married couple.

Be sure to name the gift and make a connection between it and you, whenever possible. You may be able to tell the gift-giver how you will use and enjoy it, some nice detail about it, and your appreciation for it:

Dear Janette and Derrick,

We love the waffle maker, and have, in three mornings, had buttermilk, walnut, and golden waffles. How did you possibly know that the color is spectacular in our kitchen? Here's Rick on waffle duty. See what a great match it is with the toaster, and even the wallpaper? Thank you both so much. We'll think of you with every waffle. Your thoughtfulness, gift, card, and good wishes all touched our hearts. Stomachs too!

Yours most affectionately,
Sophie and Richard

Congratulation Cards or Notes to the New Couple

I FIND IT REWARDING to cast a broad net in sending congratulations. If I know the bride well, I send a note when I hear of the upcoming marriage. (See chapter 8, Engagements.) After the wedding (usually with a gift), I send a note of congratulations and best wishes to the wedded couple. This is usually penned in a lovely greeting card.

I send a special note of congratulations to the family members I know well, and sometimes even to persons, or couples, I've just met at the wedding who will be part of the couple's new community. It's a great chance to celebrate these connections. Here are a few examples:

Dear Alice,

What a wonderful wedding service you orchestrated for your beautiful Kerry. I thought their vows were rich in meaning.

Kerry looked radiant. Knowing you these twenty years, I certainly appreciate that you are a perfectionist, but on your daughter's wedding you succeeded at the highest level. You didn't miss a single detail. I couldn't believe that every table at the sit-down dinner was festooned with scallops of tiny rose buds, and that each table had a pedestal of the loveliest arrangements of roses and ivy I've ever seen.

My, this wedding was truly lovely, one Newton and I will never forget.

We look forward to having you and the newlyweds over for a dinner party after they settle in. We'll be so happy to see the wedding photos, and hear all the behind-the-scenes stories.

Affectionately,
Adelle

Dear Nan,

Yours is only the second wedding I've ever attended where the bride and groom sang their wedding vows. It brought tears to my eyes. I appreciate now, more fully, what a perfect fit Egan is for your family. Your mother told me how you two are a match made in heaven, and now that I've heard your voices blended in song, I know that it's true.

What a bright and glorious future lies in store for your life together. How happy I am for you, and how I look forward to embracing you as a couple.

With love always,
Aunt Ermma

Dear Isiah:

What a wonderful choice you and Hannah have made in selecting each other. What a blessing that you will have each other, and what a blessing you will be to the whole family. Welcome.

With warmest regards,
Aunt Esther

Dearest Avia,

You have made your mother and grandma very proud today. You're all grown up into a fine and strong woman, and today have taken a wonderful husband we all adore. What a happy, happy day. I'm full of joy to overflowing, and I just want you to know how much the two of you, Mr. and Mrs. Bond, are loved.

Affectionately,
Grandma

Use every connection, observation, and happy emotion in expressing your good wishes to all those within the community of the new couple—that their joy may be full!

(Also see chapter 4, Thank You, and chapter 8, Engagements.)

10

Anniversaries

March 4, 1983

Dear First Lady,

I know tradition has it that on this morning I place cards—Happy Anniversary cards on your breakfast tray. But things are somewhat mixed up. I substituted a gift & delivered it a few weeks ago.

Still this is the day, the day that marks 31 years of such happiness as comes to few men. I told you once it was like an adolescent's dream of what marriage should be like. That hasn't changed.

You know I love the ranch—but these last two days made it plain I only love it when you are there. Come to think of it that's true of every place & every time. When you aren't there I'm no place, just lost in time & space.

I more than love you, I'm not whole without you. You are life itself to me. When you are gone I'm waiting for you to return so I can start living again.

Happy Anniversary & thank you for 31 wonderful years.
I love you
Your Grateful Husband
[Ronald Reagan]

MARRIAGE IN OUR POST-POST–MODERN WORLD, it often seems to me, is held together by blown kisses and Post-It notes. With all the separate demands on each partner, this union sometimes seems more like two ships crisscrossing in a stormy night than like two partners traveling on a united journey. But an anniversary is exactly the right time to celebrate a marriage, reflect on everything that is good about it, reevaluate it, and set new goals for making it a more wonderful, mystical, and sacred alliance—a shared and rich partnership between two committed people.

To Your Spouse

THERE ARE MANY VERY good reasons to write something special to your spouse on this day. Certainly you can search for a commercial greeting card that has a wonderful, appropriate message, but always compose your own message, too—short or long. To begin, start from the outside, your physical senses and experiences, then move deeper into your heart for a unique expression. This will take a little effort, so use a notebook or practice paper, and just begin writing without censoring yourself.

What you write can include something that reflects on how you two started on this journey and why. It can include something about the "us" experience you've built together; it can review your year together and the growth you've experienced; and it can express

your wishes for the year to come. No marriage has too many celebrations:

> *Has it really only been two years? I can't remember life without*
> *you. Really. You are truly sunshine to each of my days, as I knew*
> *you would be the moment I saw you and was instantly tongue-*
> *tied. Remember? You thought I was hoarse, or mute, but the truth*
> *was you just rendered me speechless. And I am still so in awe of*
> *you, I can't find words to adequately express how much I love you,*
> *and how happy I am to be married to you. . . .*

> *The seventh year of marriage is called the "itchy" year by some.*
> *But not by me. This has been the most wonderful year of my life,*
> *and one filled with more closeness than I could ever have dared*
> *hope we'd be able to realize. How wonderful it is being married*
> *to you. . . .*

> *No one gave our marriage much of a chance after that wedding*
> *ceremony: the flower girl refused to walk down the aisle, your*
> *bridesmaid fainted, my best man dropped your ring, and Aunt*
> *June fell and nearly toppled the cake. But you are now, as you*
> *were then, the love of my life . . .*

Once you get started—and don't be afraid to cross out and start
over again, since this is a rough draft—be sure the focus moves to
your spouse; your note should be about *him* or *her*. This is the person
who should be the star in your message, not you. Compare the
impact of the "me" and the "you" focuses:

Me: . . . *You mean so much to me . . .*

You: . . . *What a wonderful person you are . . .*

See the difference? Follow this up with concrete qualities that make your spouse unique:

You showed real and wonderful determination this year when you . . .

. . . What tenderness you demonstrated when Alice lost her mom. You were right there. . . .

. . . What a generous act you committed in giving up a well-earned vacation to help me with . . .

. . . You displayed the sweetest and best of motherly love in allowing Cary to . . .

. . . You overcame real adversity this year when you . . .

. . . You were so courageous in taking on . . .

Focus on your spouse and *his* or *her* contributions:

. . . Your generosity of heart in our life together is golden . . .

. . . Your selflessness is often the engine that makes our relationship run smoothly . . .

. . . At least three critical times this year it's been your determination that has pulled us through. Remember when . . .

Perhaps you'll want to focus on where you two started, how far you've come, what your spouse means to you, and where you'll go from here:

. . . Remember the vows we each wrote twenty years ago. I had no idea, really, that you would so far exceed those words . . .

. . . We said we'd have a dog in our first year, a house in our third, and a baby in our fifth. And we have. What I wasn't prepared for was how much more precious you would become in these six years as we've faced, together, the challenges of . . .

. . . I really had no idea, ten years ago, how wonderful marriage to you could be . . .

. . . May this be the year of our deepening faith in each other as we start on . . .

Take some time to polish your message. Leave it to season a bit. Reread it, even aloud, to be sure you sense that it connects and flows from those feelings you have in your heart. Deliver it with love!

To Your Parents

YOU KNOW, PERHAPS BETTER than anyone else, the unique "us" that exists between these two people, your parents, and that's why your voice at this time of special celebration is so precious. They are, of course, your parents, but write from your observations of what you see when they relate to each other. *Focus on them.* No one else can add your unique contribution to this celebration.

It can be especially meaningful for a couple to receive greetings from their children as they grow, as these can be placed in an album of memories, taken out later, reviewed by parents and children, and held close.

But it's important that you consider, *first* and *foremost*, how your parents feel about their anniversary and its celebration. I know a couple who, after forty-five years of marriage, still want their special day to remain a secret. Not even their adult children know the exact day or year they married.

I've also known exuberant grown children who insisted on having a huge celebration of fifty or a hundred people, when the celebration couple would have much preferred a quiet, family-only dinner. The parents went along with the kids' plan only to please them. This is *their* day, so be sensitive to their wishes.

For your handwritten greeting to your parents, you may wish to start by drawing on their history:

Some of my first memories are of being in the backseat of the car on a Sunday ride to Grandma's house. I loved the way you talked to each other in the front seat; and how you, Mom, would place a hand on Dad's shoulder and say, "Eddie, Sundays with you are the highlight of my week." I loved those times, and I felt so secure and loved. . . .

Dad, I remember so well that anniversary celebration when you gave Mom the charm bracelet with the two little bootie charms engraved "Jill" and "Jack." She cried for half an hour, and you, at first, looked so stricken. Then you realized how happy and touched she was. . . .

When I try to think of my very first memory of the two of you, I see you in the garden, straw hats in place, planting those "Big Boy" tomatoes. What a wonderful thing you've grown over these twenty years. . . .

I'm so happy you made me! I love you. . . . [From an eight-year-old.]

The ninth anniversary is pottery, and here's one I made for you both for a geranium. Happy wedding birthday. [Written by a ten-year-old.]

Or you may wish to use something in the present, or a future plan or goal, as a point for starting your greeting:

This is the year of the Paris anniversary, and what a place to celebrate where you met, what you loved about each other, and your plans and desires for your future together. I'm so lucky you two found each other, and I hope someday to have a love as beautiful as yours. You've shown me what marriage can be! . . .

What an exciting year this will be for you two as you set sail on your twentieth year aboard "Joy Ride." Now I know, of course, why you were so eager for me to go off to college! . . .

Putting yourself into the picture, connecting the dots between your parents and you, may be especially meaningful:

It makes no mathematical sense that a couple married only a year has a twenty-year-old daughter, but the beauty and magic of this story is how a daughter introduced her lonely father to her wonderful professor. The two liked each other immediately, fell in love, and then married. Now as you start the second year of your happily-ever-after fairy tale, I must make a little confession: I believe I'm happier than you two are. Seeing the magic you make together is more joy than I ever hoped for. Yes, I think I'm the happiest. If that's possible. I love you both. Happy anniversary. . . .

How does one couple with four children, two careers, a spoiled Airedale, and a sassy Manx manage to find a way to celebrate their anniversary? The kids pool their funds, fix dinner for themselves, and send this couple out to The Wellshire for an evening of dinner and dancing. Because you two are the greatest, and the best. We love you . . .

We may have felt while growing up that you two "double teamed" us, presenting a united front to our nagging pleas at times, like when we petitioned for a pony. But looking back we treasure the unity you always displayed. You created a loving and secure environment for us to grow up in. . . .

Watching your relationship—from inside our family—has taught me so many things. Where should I start? Maybe your example of how to discern what is important in a relationship is what I value most. I'll never forget when . . . Thank you for living such a great example . . .

To Your Friends and Relatives

NO COUPLE IS AN island, and this is also a special time for close friends and other relatives to help the couple celebrate. Certainly their wedding party should send a special greeting. It's always appropriate to recount a precious memory from the couple's history, to recall a shared experience, to toast their marriage with words of appreciation for their life together, and to conclude with wishes for future happiness. You can even use one of the traditional anniversary gift materials as a starting place. Here are those listed in *Emily Post's Etiquette*:

Year 1   Paper or plastics
Year 2   Calico or cotton
Year 3   Leather or simulated leather
Year 4   Silk or synthetic material
Year 5   Wood
Year 6   Iron
Year 7   Copper or wood
Year 8   Electrical appliances
Year 9   Pottery
Year 10   Tin or aluminum
Year 11   Steel
Year 12   Linen (table, bed, etc.)
Year 13   Lace
Year 14   Ivory
Year 15   Crystal or glass
Year 20   China
Year 25   Silver
Year 30   Pearl
Year 35   Coral and jade
Year 40   Ruby
Year 45   Sapphire
Year 50   Gold
Year 60   Diamond

It needn't be long, and it certainly may be written on a commercial greeting card, but use your knowledge of the couple to tune into a meaningful message of one-of-a-kind and personal good wishes:

Paper doesn't seem nearly sturdy enough to express the durable, loving quality of your demonstrated love, but please accept this special copy of your marriage license as our gift on your first wedding anniversary . . .

After eloping and that shaky non-honeymoon, we thought our best friends' marriage was one that wouldn't last. Congratulations, you two. You've demonstrated how to build a very special relationship. . . .

I didn't think you could take your relationship to a new level after getting married on Vail Mountain, at eleven thousand feet. But you have, and it's a joy to know you . . .

The "career couple" who were thinking about getting a dog, but didn't know if they could manage that level of commitment, have just had twins, two brothers for Amy. (And the dog is happy and well adjusted, too.) What a delight you two are. We love you both . . .

Last year it was Alaska and salmon fishing. The year before the Sandlers went to London. Next year is the "Year of the Chinese Bear," I've heard. What a wonderful way to celebrate such a great union . . .

11

Births and Adoptions

The angel that presided o'er my birth
Said, "Little creature, formed of joy and mirth,
Go love without the help of any thing on earth."
—WILLIAM BLAKE,
The Angel That Presided

THE ARRIVAL OF A CHILD is a truly joyous event, and expressing this joy to the parents—whether the new member has arrived by birth or adoption—helps to build a community around the family. It fosters an extended circle of well-wishers where everyone will feel cherished.

So many of the new parents I know have postponed this part of their lives because of marriage and career considerations. And quite a few others have endured long and difficult trials in the process of birthing or adopting a new family member. All these things work to build anticipation, and to add to making this life event a time for great celebration.

The first thing you'll want to do before dashing off a note of congratulations is gather a little information. That's what I did before writing a note to a new single mom, whose special-needs daughter, age three, had just arrived from Russia. I checked with the new grandmother first, then followed up with this:

Anna,

We're so happy you are finally—after two-and-a-half years—welcoming your daughter Natasha to heart and home in Denver. What a demonstration of love you've already showered on her just to get her here. Was there ever a more fortunate, or more deeply loved child? We seriously doubt it. What a wonderful mom Natasha has been blessed with. What a joy to see the two of you together at last.

We would like to be part of your extended family, if you'll have us. We suggest a small "family" welcoming dinner at our home on Friday evening, the 11th, at 7:00 P.M.; just a few of your friends, new aunties and uncles. We promise to keep it low-key. (We've enclosed a suggested list of guests, please add or subtract.) Maybe you'd let us all know then how we can be most helpful to you and Natasha. (We're available for Thursday afternoon strolls from three to five, too, if you'd like for us to pick Natasha up and take her for two hours once a week.)

Welcome home, Natasha! You are much loved.

Charles and Sandy

Obviously, this first note of welcome and congratulations reflects the relationship of the sender of the new parents. Every note, too, should be sensitive to other aspects of the new child's arrival and how the family feels about it.

Your note will be so much more meaningful if you find out a few details and bring them to mind before writing. Use these questions to find a starting place for your note: Is the child a boy or a girl? Did the parents know the sex of the unborn child, and did they want to know? Are there known health considerations of the infant or parents? What are the names, sex, and ages of siblings? What were you able to learn from the birth announcement that can be helpful in your writing? What special family life style, conditions, and religious beliefs affect what you should write?

If you don't know these things, and finding out might be intrusive, it's best to keep your congratulations short and general in tone. Use the information you have, and start with something like:

We were so happy to learn of the birth of your new daughter, Eliza Jane.

Welcome, Neal Bryant Coffman. What a wonderful day when a new baby arrives.

With joyful hearts we'd like to join with you in welcoming your new baby, Erin Esther.

I remember the day your mom arrived, little Jonathan Kendell Richardson. There was much celebrating that day, too. Such a beautiful baby girl she was, and such rejoicing at the Madsen home. What a wonderful family you've selected, Jonathan. I'm proud to have known three generations now, so I feel qualified to say you have been born into a marvelous and loving clan.

Once upon a time in the wonderful family of Durbins, on a magical day in June—the 15th to be exact—a new and long-awaited, very special person arrived: You, Cary Appleton Rivers. And all the family, starting with two delighted Grandmothers, went throughout the kingdom to tell the great news. (And they also went to bridge club!)

Two very special people have now become three! Happy day!

Congratulations to Other Relatives

WOULDN'T YOU BE THRILLED to receive a note of congratulations if you were a new aunt? A new sister, or brother? Certainly you would if you were a new Grandmother or Grandfather!

This is the perfect time to spread the joy, and to help encircle others (especially if they might be feeling a tiny bit out of the center of things) within the glow of this miraculous event.

The best place to start would be an older sibling. Along with every younger, new arrival is the tiniest green-eyed monster of jealousy. When my second son was born, our twenty-month-old said, while holding his brand-new brother just from the hospital, smiling, and after kissing the baby's forehead, "We don't play in the street. It's dangerous! The street is for cars. Let's go put Eric in the street." While other big brothers and sisters may be a bit more subtle, they may still feel a little bit displaced.

If an older sibling receives a special congratulations card and a small gift, it will go a great distance toward spreading the joy. If you go for a brief visit, be sure you take time and effort to include an older brother or sister, too. This would be a great time for a big brother card, and even a small gift, if you're taking one for the new family member.

An Offer to Help

IF YOU ENJOYED a close relationship with the parents before the birth or adoption, and perhaps offered after-arrival assistance, now's the time to follow up with a couple of concrete suggestions, and give legs to your words. This is especially true in the cases where older siblings are present, or when the family has just had a multiple birth.

Vague offers aren't helpful, and many times give the impression of insincerity. It will work best if you make your offer as specific as possible to avoid any misunderstanding. Make sure it is something you are willing and able to do:

May I bring over a chicken casserole on Thursday at 5:30 P.M.?

I do my grocery shopping on Monday afternoons. I'd be happy to pick up something for you and drop it by on my way home about 4 P.M. Let me know.

I'd be happy to walk Snoopy on Mondays and Wednesdays at 7:30 A.M. for the next three weeks. Give me a call if you'd like me to stop by and take her.

This is a woman who knows colic. I'd be thrilled to do walking patrol from two to four each afternoon next week. Call and I'll come over, and you can try to nap.

Why not let me drop off a take-out dinner for the next four Mondays? I can bring it by on my way home from work, about 6 P.M. Let me know if this sounds good.

Adoptions Are Very Special

FOCUS ON THE CREATION of a wonderful new family, the addition of a much-wanted and much-loved child, the happiness of the parents, and your good wishes for all of them. Don't assume people adopt only because of fertility problems. Remember, these *are* the parents of the child, so reference to "biological parents" can be offensive, as can questions about race, living conditions, and so forth.

Dear Abigail and Ross,

With so many children in the world in need of a home, how wonderful that you have the supply of love to go and find three and take them to your heart. You two are very special people, and now the parents of three daughters. How delighted we were to hear of the finally successful trip from China of Sui, Beth, and Wa Linn.

Your home must be overflowing with happiness, times three.

We eagerly await hearing all about your wonderful new family, and we're so eager to meet the girls. We know it will take a while to get settled and work out a routine, so we won't call until next week to see what a good time and arrangements for a very brief visit might be.

In the meantime, there are many happy songs of praise ascending from this home, and many prayers of thanksgiving from the loving hearts of your extended family here.

With love,
Robert and Alexa

Special Babies and Special Families

WHEN A FAMILY IS BLESSED with a child with special needs, it is even more important to be sensitive to the views and feelings of everyone involved. Knowing the parents and other relatives well is most often the key to writing something meaningful.

Don't ask. This is no time for questions. So stifle those that quickly come to mind: Is this an inherited condition? Was there a problem in delivery? What's the prognosis?

It is best to steer clear of the normal commercial baby congratulations cards, and simply write a note that indicates you want to acknowledge the baby's arrival, you are concerned, and you will keep the family in your thoughts and prayers.

Dear Meryl and Steven,

We've heard that your beloved baby, Katie Lynn, has arrived, and we understand there are some health concerns. We just want you to know that all three of you are in our thoughts and prayers each day.

If we can keep Scruffy for a couple of weeks, we would feel we are at least being a little helpful; or, if you'd like to have your telephone forwarded here for answering, we'd be pleased to answer and screen calls. Please do call on us if either of these things, or something else, would be helpful.

Your friends,
Jenn and Jack

Dear Jackie and Bruce,

Rebecca has passed on the news of Deborah's birth, congratulations to all three of you. No baby could have more wonderful parents.

Rebecca says you may be in need of consulting respiratory specialists. As you may remember, we did extensive research to find an infant pulmonary specialist after Judith was born. At the point you are ready to start your search, we would be happy to discuss our findings with you. Just give us a call. Until then, you will be constantly on our hearts and in our thoughts.

Warmly yours,
Allie and Roger

12

Life Achievements

Who will take my father's place . . . in this daily practice of the language of
the tribe? Anyone who wishes. He said once the field of writing will never be
crowded—not because people can't do important work, but because they
don't think they can.
—KIM R. STAFFORD *about his father, the poet William Stafford*
(1914–1993)

I CAN NEARLY SEE the face of my grandmother, who died when
I was two, reciting a poem in which the last line of each verse
repeated, ". . . Give them the flowers before they die." That's what
your personal note celebrating a person's life achievements can do.
My grandmother had another oft-used phrase she employed when
someone was being criticized, "Give everyone their due . . . ," and
she would follow this up by saying something nice about the
person.

". . . *that their joy may be full.*" The truth is, the only thing better
than achieving a hard-won goal is having others acknowledge and
help you celebrate. Do you have an uncle who is retiring after forty
years? A friend whose first novel is just coming out? A nephew who
will become an Eagle Scout next month—a goal he's had since his
first Cub Scout meeting? A cousin who has finally received his
Ph.D.? A friend who finished a marathon after overcoming a disabil-
ity, and years of preparation?

Life achievements imply, of course, that a high goal was set, extensive preparation was made, much effort was exerted, and the prize has finally been won. This is quite different from, say, a note of congratulations on winning the lottery, becoming employee of the week, or being crowned homecoming queen.

Writing such a note takes knowing the person, and appreciating her goals and hard work. Start by making a few notations about how the person set her goal:

I remember when Mom used to tell me, as a little girl, that you had to miss a family gathering because, as a doctor, you always put sick people first. I was disappointed then; I am awed now. It's a wonderful thing to see you being given the humanitarian award. . . .

I well remember all those weekend classes, all those missed poker parties, all those fishing trips you gave up to study; and now, David Parker, Ph.D., I salute you . . .

Your whole working life you kept alive the quiet fire of desire to serve in a foreign country in the Peace Corps. . . .

I remember the first thing you said after moving into the corner office: "Susan, I'm going to make a difference here." Let me count the ways. . . .

Let's see, how many knots, how many tent setups, how many Monday night scout meetings, and how many leadership projects has it taken to make an Eagle Scout? I remember your first pair of gold knee socks. . . .

The doctors said, after your accident, you wouldn't be able to finish high school. Remember the day you said to me, "Mom, I'm going to finish, and I'm going to finish with my class. . . ."

Recount as many of the details of the process and person's efforts as will help you to connect to the person and to connect the person to the achievement:

I remember well the Saturday afternoon when you nearly gave up, saying, "Sarah, I think this may just be too hard. . . ."

I remember watching when you entered your first triathlon, swam out into the Bay about a hundred yards, and had to turn back.

I don't know another soul who would have continued after "Black Tuesday." But you did!

Don't spare the details or the praise. Make them as big as the achievement will allow. And don't dilute the message with anything else—make sure to keep the achiever the star:

Jennifer Beasley, you are truly an outstanding person. Who else would have . . .

Anyone else would have thrown in the towel after the first brutal critique. But not you . . .

Bruce, you are the most courageous person I know. Who else would have . . .

Close with a warm hope for the future, and perhaps even the suggestion of many more possibilities and achievements in the future.

With all you've accomplished, you could certainly just spend all your time now taking bows, but somehow I'm sure you've outlined some new goal . . .

Here's to your new beginning, and to the next life achievement you have on your "To Do" list.

Resting on your laurels? Not a chance. What marvelous new goal have you set for yourself?

(Also see chapter 5, Congratulations; chapter 13, Rites of Passage and Life Events; and chapter 16, Appreciation.)

13

Rites of Passage and Life Events

To everything there is a season, and a time to
every purpose under the heaven.
A time to be born, and a time to die; a time to
plant, and a time to pluck up that which is planted;
—ECCLESIASTES 2:16

ENRICHING IMPORTANT RITES of passage—both religious
and social—with your own handwritten personal note is a wonderful
way to help make the event more meaningful for the celebrant, family, and friends. It's also a wonderful way to reaffirm your connections to the celebrant, and to create a lasting memory.

Religious Rites of Passage

BIRTH CEREMONY
(Christening, Dedication, Baptism, Briss, and so forth)

EVERY FAITH CELEBRATES the birth of a baby as a very special
event. Although the form may differ substantially, I've always found
that the parents and other family members find their joy multiplied
by expressions of congratulations, and acknowledgments of their
commitment to safeguard and instruct the new child in a path of
religious faith.

Usually these ceremonies are handled with informal invitations, extended only to very close family and very special friends. Gifts, if any, are usually small items of a religious nature, or something that has import for the child's future, like stock, bonds, or money. These are only given if you are very close to the family, and should always reflect your relationship to them, within the scope of what you can afford.

As part of your birth congratulations, or in a separate note, it will be meaningful to share in the celebration of this birth event. If you are of the same faith, this will be easy; but if not, you may still state something general like:

How wonderful, too, that Roxanne Elizabeth has been entrusted to two wonderful parents who value the role of faith in her life . . .

Your mother told me the dedication ceremony was beautiful . . .

Daniel and I feel humbled to have been selected to be Christine's godparents. With joy, we commit to help guide her in the path of faith. It was a very moving and solemn moment for us to take part in her . . .

Quotes from the Bible, Torah, or other religious books are often used, as are quotes from the church or religious leaders. The more you know about the family's religion, the easier and more meaningful your communication will be. Don't, however, borrow terms from a faith you don't share. (See the box on page 115.)

CEREMONIES OF FAITH

IF YOU DON'T share the same beliefs as the celebrating family, it's best to keep your message focused on the celebrant and his or her

Special Birth Ceremonies

CHRISTIAN

A ceremony of baptism, christening, or dedication may take place immediately after birth, or later. These ceremonies generally focus on welcoming the infant and dedicating the newborn and parents to the child's life in the faith.

JEWISH

Boys are named, and undergo the circumcision ceremony, brith milah (brit in Yiddish), on the eighth day after birth. This is usually held in the morning hours, and is attended by close family and friends.

Girls have a naming ceremony, which is held between the first Sabbath after birth to several weeks afterward, but within the first month.

HINDU

The naming ceremony takes place when the baby is between six and eight months of age, and takes place at home. It also denotes the ability of the child to eat solid food, and is called the "rice-eating ceremony."

ISLAMIC

Newborns are honored with an *akikah ceremony*, which varies widely by cultural influence.

feelings. It's always appropriate to recognize the joy of the child, and the deep significance of this event.

First Communion and Confirmation

IN THE ROMAN CATHOLIC CHURCH, the First Communion signifies that a child of six or seven has completed a course of study (usually a year), and is prepared to participate in this important sacrament of the Church. The Roman Catholic Confirmation signifies that the child has "come of age" and now has adult responsibility in the Church. This ceremony usually takes place between the ages of twelve and fifteen.

Protestant children may have First Communion, Confirmation, Initiation, or Statement of Faith ceremonies, separately or in combination, and these may occur at a variety of ages, though usually after age seven.

I suggest you learn something about the ceremony and its significance before writing to the celebrant. It may be best even to ask another member of the congregation, or someone in the family, before writing.

I often write a very brief and simple message, based on what I've learned about how the child feels about the step she's taken, and what I've learned about the significance of the ceremony:

Chloe, what an important and holy day for you, making your First Communion. It is truly a day you will always remember, and one of the most important days of your life . . .

Happy is the girl whose heart is full of faith; and we are so happy for you on this very special day.

God's blessings on you as you begin your life of faith in the Church.

*You have taken a very important step on the path of faith today,
and our hearts are full of joy and rejoicing. . . .*

Bar Mitzvahs and Bat Mitzvahs

THE AGE-OLD PRACTICE (at least since the Middle Ages) of welcoming a Jewish boy of thirteen years into his adult place of responsibility within the Jewish community is called the bar mitzvah, or "son of the commandment" in Hebrew. It takes place on the first Saturday after the young man's thirteenth birthday. The bat mitzvah, "daughter of the commandment," is a much newer tradition, having originated in the twentieth century. (It still isn't practiced by many Orthodox Jewish congregations.) Girls may be twelve years and one day old, or thirteen.

The ceremony is proceeded by many months of religious training, and involves having the child read from the Torah in the synagogue, and/or the Haphtarah (a reading from Prophets) as part of the Saturday worship service. The child then makes a speech about the significance of attaining religious adulthood.

Formal invitations and replies are usually sent, and gifts of lasting value, often money, are given. The party has taken on the dimensions of a great social, as well as religious, event.

This is a wonderful time, I think, to speak to the young person (formerly a child) about the deep significance of the ceremony, the outstanding accomplishment he or she has made, and his or her progress and growth. You may also want to reaffirm connections, mention the joy and pride family and friends feel, and extend your wishes for his or her future. Your message should, of course, reflect your connection to the celebrant and the family. Start your message with any of these thoughts:

*Mazel tov! We know how hard you studied, and how seriously
you regard your new status in the community . . .*

What a beautiful ceremony, and what a wonderful time to become a young Jewish woman. . . .

A very wise person said to me on my bat mitzvah day, "Sarah, follow the example of your grandmother, Ruth." You, too, have some wonderful examples to follow starting with your grandmother. I know she wouldn't tell you, but did you know that she . . .

Social Rites of Passage

SOCIAL RITES OF PASSAGE are rich with the significance of entering a new stage in life. These offer the opportunity to celebrate a common heritage, shared experiences, new beginnings, and family ties.

In writing your note, focus on the eagerly awaited event, the celebrant's increased maturity, her wonderful progress, and the future setting and reaching of some of her goals:

Alison, I simply can't believe you are fifteen. I know older relatives always say things like, "It seems like just yesterday you were a tiny girl," but it's true. We loved you as a tiny girl of one and two, and dared not hope you would develop into such a fine young and accomplished woman. But you have . . .

Sweet sixteen, and what a marvel! . . .

Eighteen years old, and every bit as lovely a person as you are a beauty . . .

If only we would have known that you would reach eighteen so soon, we'd have frozen a few of those days when you were four

Special Social Rites of Passage for Young Women

QUINCEAÑERA

This Hispanic or Latino celebration held for a girl reaching fifteen reaffirms her vows, and welcomes her into the Catholic young adult community. The party held afterward is popular in Central America, Cuba, Puerto Rico, and in Mexican populations in both Mexico and the United States. It's a sort of debutante dance or big party, complete with gala attire. "Congratulations" (*Felicidades*) is the best form of greeting.

SWEET-SIXTEEN PARTY

To celebrate a young woman's reaching a milestone of her sixteenth birthday, this event denotes her new status as a young adult, and may be as fancy as a co-ed dance, or as informal as an all-girls slumber party.

DEBUTANTE EVENT

These events or parties denote a young woman's eighteenth birthday and her entry into society: "coming out." They may range from formal charity balls (introducing a number of debutantes) to informal afternoon teas.

and holding those fabulous tea parties. I can hardly wait to hear
what you'll be doing this year . . .

Family Celebrations and Rites of Passage

FAMILY CELEBRATIONS CAN HELP create a rich texture of
family identity, and a secure sense of belonging. All such celebrations and rites distinguish a family, and enrich the human experience, reinforce bonds, and are life-affirming. Write a personal note to
those being honored. Suggest older family members bring albums of
photos and identify family members. Ask someone to start developing a family history and family tree (with or without photos), take
videos and show those of prior get-togethers, bring family folklore
tales and stories to tell, and assemble a family book of favorite
recipes.

Communicating about these things between get-togethers will
help connect family members of all generations.

14

Welcome

True friendship's laws are by this rule express'd,
Welcome the coming, speed the parting guest.
—HOMER

WHEN WE MOVED into an Indianapolis neighborhood many years ago, four new neighbors and the "Welcome Wagon" representative dropped by the day after we arrived. There was a pot of soup and homemade bread made by the woman next door, a plate of cookies from across the street, and a basket full of business references, coupons, and other giveaways from the Welcome Wagon representative. It helped to abate my homesickness for the East Coast. Some of these fine, old-fashioned acts of civility and hospitality are quickly becoming a thing of the past. What a pity.

It doesn't take much time or effort to telephone and introduce yourself to a new neighbor, or to stop by after the moving truck has pulled away with a small basket of fresh-baked cookies and a note of welcome. Following up with a written note containing several recommendations for neighborhood businesses, babysitters, and services, like lawn care, will go a long way toward establishing friendly relationships. The same is true of new members to your garden club, book club, gourmet group, Junior League, university alumni group, or the press club you belong to. Sometimes we extend this kind of courtesy, and more, to business contacts, but neglect our social contacts.

A welcome note is best sent immediately. Send yours in that first week, and start with an enthusiastic welcome. You'll want to keep the message simple, and focused on key information the person will find useful to know. Say something positive about what you've found beneficial, perhaps what you most wanted to know when you were in that person's shoes. Offer future help, if that's appropriate—you'll be wise to make it explicit to avoid any confusion. Close with a statement of your anticipation for a future relationship.

Here are a few examples:

Dear Mabel and Myron,

Welcome to our neighborhood! I think you'll find our little cul-de-sac a quiet and congenial group. Each July 4 we do a neighborhood picnic, then gather to watch fireworks from one of the balconies.

We have some outstanding nearby services, which I've listed on the attached sheet. I've also included several recommendations for services we particularly like to use, including the information you requested about shoe repair, cleaners, and a butcher shop.

We've lived here fifteen years, and hope to be here another fifteen. It's a great neighborhood. We look forward to getting to know you.

> *Warmly,*
> *Bibbi and Dwer Stevens*

Dear Ellen,

How nice to meet you today at the Woman's Press Club. I joined last year, and have found it a wonderful sisterhood of giving members, willing to share information and contacts.

I would especially recommend the "Books I Love" group that meets the first Monday of each month. These wise women offer special insights into some of our best current literature. And through this group I've found several wonderful friends.

I look forward to seeing you at the next meeting, September 15. Meanwhile, if I can give you any more information about the group, please call me at: (344) 555-1332.

Sincerely,
Imma Russell

A follow-up call a few days after your note is received will indicate real interest and caring.

15

Happy Holidays

Life is short. Make it a celebration!
—ANONYMOUS

HOLIDAYS WITHOUT THE PERSONAL GREETINGS of family and friends aren't really holidays at all. Consider your own experience: Is Mother's Day really Mother's Day if your children don't remember? Or, if you don't remember your mom? What about Father's Day? Even New Year's has limited significance if it isn't an occasion for sharing and personal best wishes from those we know and love. And certainly we're enriched by sharing religious holidays with others of the same faith.

Just think about it. There are 365 days each year, and only about a dozen are holidays—a time for special celebrations. It's a thought I often have when I hear people grousing about having to get ready for the holidays, including the effort of sending holiday cards. Bah humbug! Without going overboard, we should use our holidays wisely and well to celebrate with those we know and love.

Christmas

FOR CHRISTIANS WHO CELEBRATE the birth of Jesus Christ, this is one of the holiest days of the year. It not only signifies the possibility of redemption, but the promise of eternal life. The birth of Jesus is a divine miracle signifying God's love for, and gift to, humanity. It's the central theme of this holiday, though celebrations through the centuries have added many customs to the season. Some of them, like the Christmas tree and Santa Claus, are even pagan in origin.

Christian families around the world have also added their own, special traditions, weaving them in, giving a deep and heartfelt personal significance to this holiday. It's this combination of the traditional and the personal that has created the wonderful tapestry of observations we have today.

One of the best parts of Christmas, for me, is embracing family and friends. Its starts with, and hinges upon, sending and receiving personal greetings. Some years I've displayed them on long ribbons hung festively from the tops of doorways, intertwined with strands of garland. Other years I've taken out the greeting cards from the previous year, and helped the children make Christmas tree decorations out of them, as well as handmade cards for the current year's celebration. This year I used a large ceramic bowl, made by my son, to collect the Christmas cards after we've opened them and read them to the whole family. I love to watch the bowl fill up with holiday greetings. I'm very disappointed if I open an envelope and the card contains only a prepared message and the signature of the sender. Worse still are those few that arrive with typeset signatures! How antiseptic and cold.

The greetings I especially treasure are the ones from people I love, but don't often get to see. And, although I could pick up the telephone and talk to them (or perhaps leave a message on their voice mail), I love getting their personal notes. All the better if the envelope contains a family "newsletter," with lots of grist about what they've all been up to. Of course it's great to have the newsletter end with a handwritten message to our particular family.

Yes, I want to know how the children are doing. (I'd even like a few pictures.) I want to know about the careers of friends and relatives, what kind of volunteer activities they've been up to, and major and minor changes in their beliefs and outlooks. I have a vested interest: I care.

I have a friend—a former neighbor—who each year sends a card with a family portrait slipped into a card cover. Inside is a newsy letter on festive stationery. It relates how the twins are starting kindergarten this year, what their favorite activities are, and several "life lessons" the kids and parents have taught each other. There is a funny story or two, as well. Strange, but I realized that I know this family much better through these yearly newsletters than I did when I saw them in the neighborhood several times a week!

We do our own version of this Christmas greeting, too. In fact, I save pictures from events throughout the year, clip them down to size, and paste a collage on the front and back of our newsletter. Our list of recipients includes family, friends, and neighbors. (We have a separate list for work associates, as our newsletter doesn't go to people with whom we have only a work relationship.)

I also use our newsletter to set up get-togethers for the coming year. Last year I wrote to Florida friends we haven't seen for two years, "We are going to be in Tampa in January, between the 15th and the 20th. We'll be attending a conference, but would love to get together for dinner and catch-up. How about dinner on the 18th?" To another friend I wrote, "Are you coming to Vail to ski again this season? Let's plan to meet there again in mid-February."

One year I didn't do a newsletter and received dozens of comments registering sincere disappointment and requests to be put back on our list. "Please renew my subscription . . ." came another note.

Getting Started

WHEN WRITING A SEASONAL NEWSLETTER for an extended list of family and friends, be sure to create different versions appropriate to the recipients. Second, the "news" should be primarily about yourself and your spouse; others, even your children, may not want to be featured without their knowledge and permission. Include the kids and make it a family project, if possible. And don't forget to add a personal note of greeting that connects you and the recipient, and includes a greeting of celebration.

Think of Christmas as a season and not just a day. Plan ahead, start early, and allow yourself lots of time to send out those personal greetings. You can even write them weeks ahead, and mail them all at once. Look for the joy in writing each and every one. Don't panic if you don't get them all in the mail by December 10. Your best wishes will be just as warmly received if they arrive on December 28. Or January 5.

Be sure to focus on the recipient when selecting the greeting card you send. To your Jewish friends and others who observe some of the festivities of the season but don't celebrate the birth of the Christ child, send general "happy holiday" or "season's greetings" cards, not religious ones. This also applies when you're uncertain of the belief systems of business associates and others on your list.

It's appropriate in all your greetings to use the spirit of the season to write a message of thankfulness and joy. This is also a time to warmly appreciate family and friends.

What a year! As you know, this is the year Robin and Reggie joined our family, filling our hearts with joy. After ten months, we can't remember life without them. And we couldn't have made it through their many health problems without the love and support and caring assistance of all of you. Thank you, one and all. What a miraculous and merry, merry Christmas this is. Joyful greetings from our home to yours. Here we all are in our holiday best!

To this prepared note, my friend and new mother hand-wrote:

I know we've told you this, but it bears repeating. Carson and I will never forget those rides you gave us to the hospital. You two numbered among our biggest blessings of the year, and as we give thanks for the gift of eternal life, we also give thanks for you and your example of the Christian faith in action.

I can never do Christmas without remembering the one we spent on campus because we couldn't afford the trip home. Remember our "Charlie Brown" tree with the aluminum foil, doilies (from the cafeteria), construction paper, and popcorn decorations? I've never had another quite so special. I can't wait to get together in February to really catch up. Until then, love, joy, and the peace of this blessed season to Dan, Cindy, and you.

Hanukkah (Chanukkah)

THIS EIGHT-DAY CELEBRATION begins on the 25th day of the Hebrew month, usually taking place in early to mid-December (dates vary on the calendar). The holiday commemorates the ancient

Jewish military victory of approximately 163 B.C.E., when the Maccabees defeated the Syrians, who were trying to eradicate Judaism.

This is a time to hold close and dear all those who are loved, so it's also appropriate to celebrate by writing a special greeting that can create a long-cherished memory, even a recounting of previous years and celebrations. One woman's children make a family album with each year's celebration recorded. They call their book "Sarah and Ruth's Hanukkah Memories." It's shared with all the relatives and friends every year.

Regardless of your religious faith, your personal greetings may connect you to friends and family members at this time. One Christian woman wrote to a Jewish friend, "Our wishes for love and peace in the world, and in all of our hearts, as you celebrate this Hanukkah season."

Kwanzaa

INTENDED TO CONNECT AFRICAN AMERICANS to their African heritage, this celebration was inaugurated in 1966 as a seven-day season to celebrate the unique combination of histories. The celebration week starts on December 26, and the consecutive days are specified to honor the individual and community virtues of unity, self-determination, responsibility and collective work, cooperative economics and interdependence, purpose, creativity, and faith.

Personal greetings for Kwanzaa are best focused on points of shared history, community unity, and present connections. It's always proper to tell people how special they are, and what they mean to you, as one African-American man I know wrote to his nephew:

Clarence, Your work as a volunteer at the community youth center this year has been vital to creating unity in the neighborhood.

The way you've put your heritage into practice is beautiful. I look forward to dinner at your house during the celebration next week, and I'll want to hear all about the center.

New Year's

I'M ALWAYS AMAZED at the New Year's clamor at the health club, with new members signing up for diet programs and self-improvement classes. It seems that around the world people love the chance to start a new year fresh with new resolve, and that's a good place to start your personal note. It's also great to tie in a common history or interest.

New Year's is also a time to evaluate, reprioritize, and set new goals; but the best part of a new year is turning over a new leaf. There are a number of relatives and friends I always send a New Year's greeting to, and most of them are people who don't celebrate the religious holidays. A few are relatives or friends who do, but this gives us one more point of connection.

It's a great time to include some words of wisdom, or a meaningful quote. Sometimes just a few lines of a bright and shining greeting card says what you want:

Evan and Fiona, You're never far from our thoughts. We're so excited for you with the huge challenges you're undertaking this year in Greece. All our best wishes that it will be your best year yet.

Diane and Len: We have resolved to get together more this year. We miss seeing you. I'll call you in a couple of weeks when we're back in town, and we'll coordinate our calendars. We can hardly wait to hear what you've got planned.

Susanne, What an exciting year for you with your new book coming out this spring! Our best wishes for a blockbuster year. It couldn't happen to a more deserving person.

Make it personal and brief, and include something that anticipates a future relationship.

Mark and Ann, What would make the prospects of the new year even better is getting to spend time with you two! We're quickly approaching that season called "spring skiing." Any chance you would be up for renewing that downhill competition and evening card games we so enjoyed last year? We'd love to have you join us at the condo March 10–12. Our best wishes for a fantastic year, and just a bit more of it spent together!

Valentine's Day

IT ISN'T JUST FOR lovers anymore. Why not return to some of the fun and anticipation of those grade school days when everyone brought a cute or silly-but-fun little valentine to school for each person in the class and stuffed them into that special, big red box the kids had all worked together to decorate?

Of course, it's always nice to get that one very special, gooey and romantic valentine, too—the one that is slipped under the big satin bow atop the heart-shaped box of candy, or under that little jewelry box. A romantic candlelight dinner and a very special card, inscribed with a special personal message, certainly melts the heart.

My own bent in greetings runs more to the humorous, especially for messages to young members of the family. I've even borrowed from Dr. Seuss or Mother Goose to add a few lines of greeting aimed at fun and frivolity, as well as making it a special day. Take out an old book of nursery rhymes and give it a try. Slip in a dollar bill, a chocolate sucker, or a little sheet of paste-on (wash-off) tattoos.

For that special greeting to a lover, you can't go wrong quoting from the works of one of the love masters, like Elizabeth Barrett Browning's timeless favorite, "How do I love thee, Let me count the ways . . . ," or something less well worn; but always include a few original lines from your own heart, no matter how perfect the message of the greeting card. (And credit the original author when you use a selection.)

Easter

FOR THOSE OF THE Christian faith, this is the most holy day of the year, signifying God's redemption of man and the promise of eternal life. There's certainly no better occasion to send a personal greeting between people who share these beliefs. It can make this season of celebration even more special when family and friends get together for remembering this day.

Usually this holiday season is filled with many special events: church services, wonderful dramatic programs, and beautiful music. All of these events may be enriched with your personal greeting that emphasizes the significance of the season and makes a plan for getting together.

Like many religious holidays, we have added to the original significance with other rituals and festivities, like the giving and receiving of Easter baskets (usually candy), egg hunts—like the one staged each year on the White House lawn—and, of course, the tradition of women and girls buying and wearing a new Easter bonnet.

To a young family member, I combined some of the meaning of the day with some of the "lighter" practices:

Molly, What a special day for you—a wonderful pink and frilly Easter bonnet, an egg hunt, and new patent Mary Janes! Still, it's most precious to celebrate God's gift of eternal life on this most holy day.

Celebrations of the Seasons

CELEBRATIONS THAT MARK the beginning of the seasons aren't as much in fashion in this country as in others, but I got a new and wonderful vision of how festive and lovely these can be when my husband and I visited Stockholm and participated in the many delights of the solstice celebration. There were traditional costumed dancers, folktales told and acted out, elaborate customs and disguises, silly songs, May pole dances, special music of the season, and little girls going through daisy fields picking their flowers and weaving them together into laurels they wore on their hair.

May Day does get a little attention in this country, and it's a wonderful time to send family, friends, and neighbors greetings that note the renewal of life in the spring. Try a rendition of one of the odes to spring, or add your own creative spin to something that sings the praises of the season:

Krissie, April showers bring May flowers, and I'm sure you're busily transplanting and fertilizing, weeding and smiling all day long as you toil in your wonderful garden. In your yard, all things are green and beautiful. You're the best gardener I know. Happy May Day.

You might also slip into the envelope a small gift like a packet of special seeds. My little packets of wildflowers have been well received.

Celebrations for Those Who Keep Us Safe

SINCE THE ATTACK ON the United States, we've all come to a new realization about and appreciation for people in uniform who risk their lives for us in an effort to maintain our safety and safeguard our freedoms.

Anytime, or on Veterans' Day, Memorial Day, or a local or regional day set aside for remembering, take the time to write a personal note to someone you know who has served in the armed forces, or who works for public safety as a firefighter or police officer. Your notes can reference the special and historical meaning of the day, then offer a special thank you.

Mother's Day

> When it came, that last breath, it was as though a lamp in whose circle of light I had lived all my life had been extinguished. Now I was free to live anywhere. In the dark.
>
> —RICHARD SELZER,
> *about his mother, Gertrude*

IF LIFE IS A CELEBRATION, certainly it should start with an expression of love and appreciation on Mother's Day. One of the very best Mother's Day cards I ever received was the one my sons made themselves out of burgundy construction paper ("Sorry, Mom, all the red was gone"). Their labored message was simply: "We love you" in wobbly big letters.

Inside were three mismatched and ragged "Love Coopons": one for breakfast in bed; one for weeding the flowerbed; and one for polishing my shoes. Not only did the card represent their work together, but their continued care and effort when I cashed in my "Love Coopons" created opportunities for them to do extra acts of affection.

It's a wonderful principle I've tried to repeat: give a gift of love and care that reflects a tiny bit of the character of a mother's heart. And try to spread the day throughout the year.

There is no shortage of mother poems and verses that can be the starting point for thoughtful reflection and inspiration. Remember the single focus of your message: Mom.

A recurring lament of many Moms of adult kids is the lack of time spent with their children. That can be the best gift: enclose a coupon for a two-hour lunch; a three-hour shoe-shopping extravaganza (her shoes, you carry the bags); an afternoon tea; breakfast for just the two of you; a photography class you can take together; or a play or movie you know she will enjoy seeing with you.

You might even get her a rose bush that you name "Mother's Day (year) Rose," and use it as a start-up for a project—to learn and compare notes about growing roses. Let your love and imagination turn to something you know *she'll* enjoy.

> *Mom,*
> *Roses are red*
> *Violets are blue*
> *Nothing compares with*
> *Having a mother like you.*
>   *Love,*
>   *Douglas*

Dearest Mom,
   I don't know why it has taken me so long to appreciate all you have been and are: a kind and loving advocate, a cheerleader, and certainly a wonderful role model.

You've been strong when others folded, humble when you had ample reason to boast, kind and forgiving when others would have been focused on revenge, and loving when others acted the opposite.

You're the most wonderful person I know, and I love you with all of my heart. Thanks for being my Mom!

Always your daughter,
Ruby

Dear Mom,

You're the person who was always available whenever your family needed anything; always out in front with a great example of how to conduct oneself in adversity; and always ready with a kind word when someone needed one (even if she didn't always deserve it). You're my hero!

Thanks for being there.

And speaking of being there: Some of my fondest memories of our times together are those after-school snacks, when you'd have coffee and I'd have milk and cookies. Well, here are a few of your favorites I baked especially for you, Mom, and a couple of new ones I'm sure you'll love, too. I'll call you at milk-and-cookies time each Thursday afternoon for one of those Mom-and-daughter chats that are still one of the truly best times in life.

Happy Mother's Day. I love you, Mom.

Your loving daughter,
Jennifer

For Your Stepmom

Dearest Mom,

I finally know why they call it "stepmom." It's because my love for you has grown in steps. And now all I know is that I love you deeply.

You've made Dad, Tracy, and me a happy, amalgamated and loving family together with you, Alex, and Greg.

Your Stepson,
Andrew

Dear Jenny,

Birth moms, of course, are wonderful, and I love mine very much, but I've always felt that you, Stepmom, have a much more demanding and difficult job, because you had to learn to love me when I came as part of the package. (And that first year I wasn't very lovable.)

What a wonderful job you've done. Thank you for all your love. I love you.

Devotedly,
Susan

Mom Two,

I know I've been quite a handful this year. But that doesn't mean I don't appreciate all your efforts. Thank you for hanging in there with me.

Jennifer

For Your Mother-in-Law

MOMS-IN-LAW CAN sometimes get the short end of the stick. Although they aren't your birth mother, they deserve your love, kindness, and appreciation. As one psychologist put it, "It's important to realize that your mother-in-law will always be your husband's mother. Embrace her, determine to build a great relationship with her, and extend every loving courtesy."

For her Mother's Day greeting, start with a connecting message about what a wonderful person she is to have raised such a wonderful son. You can even mention specific characteristics and examples.

I know that Kevin first learned the generous spirit he has shown in helping me with graduate school from you. . . .

I see your caring instruction in the way Garson is so willing to take on the two A.M. feedings . . .

There aren't words to express what a wonderful person you created in Stephen . . .

Offer a gift of your time:

I'd love to take you to tea at the Brown on Thursday . . .

I'm coming through Chicago on a business trip next month. Could we have a late Mother's Day lunch downtown on Wednesday the 12th, say 12:30 P.M.? You pick the spot, I'll treat. I'd love to hear about your trip.

For the woman who has everything, here's that cat toy I'm sure Whiskers will love as much as Miss Sniff does.

I want to express my love and admiration for raising a wonderful son! I look forward to growing our relationship, too, into something unique and wonderful.

For Your Grandmother

FOR THIS MOTHER'S DAY I created a Dr. Seuss–like book of the story of my boys' days at Grandma's and Grandpa's house. Before I started, I asked my mother to share with me her stories (not that I hadn't heard them more than once). I also made a collage of photos for the book, which featured camping trips, fishing, ice cream making, roughhousing, and lots of other memories of the boys' visits.

The book went to my mother for Mother's Day, and I made a copy for each son. Yes, it was a lot of work, but it was worth every minute spent. My mother was delighted, and the boys love their books, too. But one of the greater benefits is that it has sparked a new view of their grandparents for the boys, and has served as a continuing connection, facilitating more dialogue between them.

Observe special celebration days for grandparents. Look up the official days, or set them in your own family, and send a special greeting. Because children grow so quickly, once a year is not often enough. Involve your children early. Little ones who don't write yet can dictate their messages. Include pieces of schoolwork, and a few lines about soccer and swimming, birthday parties, scouts, and other activities.

Father's Day

ALTHOUGH THEY OFTEN DON'T say so, dads love to know they're loved and appreciated, but if you have "macho" men in your family, keep a lid on the pomp and dazzle. I'm guessing that if your gift is the latest book by his favorite author, a fishing lure, a package of golf balls (from St. Andrews in Scotland), or a "Dad and Me" photo, he'll be quietly delighted. If you opt for "Love Coupons" (a round of golf, or a car wash, for example), he will cherish the thought, even if he doesn't cash them in.

Dad and Granddad will always enjoy a shared happy experience of the past year as a starting place for your greeting. They will also enjoy making the day a get-together. And write that special message to Dad. It will mean the most.

Dad,
Roses are red
Violets are blue
I'm so happy
to have a wonderful Dad like you!
You're the best! I love you.
                                        Mark

Dad,
   This hasn't been a happy year for any of us, and at times I've been pretty mad at you. So when I started thinking about Father's Day, I couldn't really get very excited about it. Then I got to

thinking about other Father's Days, like our dads' camp-out three years ago. And our Breckenridge hike last year. And all the other times. You're still my dad, and I love you.

Your son,
James

Shared Dads and Stepdads

I KNOW A NUMBER OF MEN who share custody of their children with an ex-spouse, and in some cases, a new stepparent, and it seems to me that this special arrangement makes Father's Day even more important to acknowledge.

Stepfathers, too, should be included in the celebration. For either dad, use a simple, short, heartfelt greeting focused on him and your relationship—with or without a commercial card:

Jim,
The fishing trip to Green River was one of our best, don't you think? You're the best fisherman and the best Dad I know. I'm so glad you're mine! (This coupon is good for two packed lunches for a fishing trip in June.)

Scott

For Other Parenting People

WE ALL KNOW "MOMS" AND "DADS" who don't happen to have children of their own. I think of all those single friends who are "big brothers" and "big sisters" to pre- and teenagers, those who do mentoring, serve as scout leaders, help in school reading programs, and serve in after-school programs. Their parenting roles are tougher in many respects because of the concern and time required to perform these caring acts. Wouldn't it be nice to remember them on this special day? Try a simple, brief message:

> *Dear Nan,*
>
> *For all those times you've shown a mother's heart and committed those caring maternal acts, I just want to say Happy Mother's Day. I appreciate your full and sharing heart.*
>
> *Rose*

Jewish Holidays

ROSH HASHANAH IS the Jewish religious New Year that commemorates the creation of the world (over 5,800 years ago). This holiday occurs the first and second days of the Hebrew month of *Tishrei*, falling on dates between mid-September and mid-October. The traditional greeting for this holiday is "Happy New Year," or in Hebrew, "Shana Tovah." The ten days following this day are set aside for worship and introspection, and culminate in The Day of Atonement, Yom Kippur.

Sending greetings to those of Jewish faith is a wonderful way to remember Rosh Hashanah, and the greetings should be reflective and brief:

> *We treasure our friendship with you, especially as we reflect upon this past year and welcome a new one. Our wishes for a wonderful new year.*

Reflecting on the sadness of this year makes us value, more than ever, your love and friendship. Our best wishes for the new year.

Happiness and health to you, our treasured family.

Yom Kippur is a day for reflection, prayer, and formal repentance of sins committed during the year. The greeting for this day is "Have an easy fast" or "Happy New Year." It's a day those of the Jewish faith abstain from work and fast from sundown to nightfall of the following day.

Your greeting can't be duplicated by anyone else because it comes from you. Personalize it with your own special style, and focus it on the person(s) you're writing to, tying it to the holiday. It will be the perfect recipe to make the celebration sweeter, for both your recipient and yourself.

16

Appreciation

Apt words have power to assuage
The tumors of a troubled mind.
—JOHN MILTON

12-6-91
The Honorable Sherwood L. Boehlert
U.S. House of Representatives
Washington, D.C. 20515

Dear Sherry:
I won't reply to every point in your good letter, but I really appreciated it.
I know that this economy will turn. I know our staff changes will help quell the attacks John was under. And I darn sure am not down. I'm used to the heat and I plan to be in the kitchen for 5 more years.
With friends like you—I will be. All Best from a grateful
George Bush [Sr.]

A NOTE OF APPRECIATION is best served up as a surprise to someone who isn't expecting it, but whose efforts are exemplary—maybe even someone who does an ordinary job in an extraordinary manner. I recently met a friend I hadn't seen for months, and during our conversation I asked if she was still volunteering at a women's crisis center as well as delivering meals several times a week to people stricken with AIDS.

"Of course," she answered.

I know she has been doing these two jobs for more than ten years, and I also know the people she helps appreciate her efforts. And so do I. Although I'm not involved with either of these two particular charities, I sat down and wrote a short note of appreciation:

> *Dear Alice,*
>
> *The world would be a much better place if we all followed your fine example of selfless care of the wounded, weak, and ill. You are truly an inspiration.*
>
> *I know how appreciated your efforts are by those you minister to, but I just want to say how much I appreciate you, too. You've spurred me to think about my own volunteering, to reevaluate and increase it.*
>
> *You're making a difference.*

There are many people who need to hear how much we appreciate them—those who contribute directly to our lives, and those who contribute to others' lives. Teachers who are doing an outstanding job need to hear from us. We all, of course, have many reasons to let soldiers, firefighters, and policemen know how we appreciate the tough jobs they do every day.

It's also important to let employees know that you appreciate their outstanding efforts. When a secretary puts in a week of overtime hours to get ready for a deadline, when a business colleague refers a client, or when a committee chairperson authors an outstanding report, a handwritten note of appreciation is a great way to express how you feel.

If you begin with the point of appreciation, the rest will flow easily. Make your note brief and sincere, and express your feelings in your own voice.

Your contribution to the new employee hiring policy is one of the best I've seen in ten years with this company.

Your unique insight into employee tardiness helped the committee do a much better job than any of us expected.

Your volunteer work as treasurer for the association for the past three years has saved the homeowners from overexpenditures on many occasions, the latest being the resurfacing of the street . . .

You've not only been Keith's "Big Brother" hero, you're the one who helped him believe he could make it into Dartmouth.

If it's appropriate, offer to reciprocate, then end with a reference to the future:

Please call on me when you need the latest figures for the Grey Report. I certainly look forward to our next opportunity to work together.

I can never repay you, of course, but I want you to know you've helped create hope and joy where there was despair. I hope you'll allow me to help you next month with the writing project. . . .

Devin,
*   I know you had to cancel your plans to see the Rockies play, and give up your tickets to make sure the sales report got finished while I was in Memphis. It was way beyond the call of duty for*

you to step in for me when I got stranded at the airport. I appreciate your sacrifice.

Will you be my guest for the Braves game on the 12th?

I'm also looking forward to doing a good deed for you in the upcoming months. I'd be pleased to be transportation coordinator for the Eagles if you'd like.

Kind regards,

Bill

17

Just Because You're You Notes

Let us all then leave behind letters of love and friendship, family and devotion, hope and consolation, so that future generations will know what we valued and believed and achieved.

—MARIAN EDELMAN,
From the Foreword of *Letters of a Nation*

I ARRIVED HOME from several days away, and opened the mailbox on my way in. It's a trained response—one part steeling myself against bills or bad news, and two parts anticipation. As usual, there were the four or five catalogs, but more annoying were the newspaper fliers I immediately deposited in the recycling bin. I quickly sorted through the remaining mail. Looking for what? What is it I always hope to see? A personal note.

Ahhh, there amongst fifty pieces of mail was a single lush, creamy envelope with small and careful swirls of script across the front. One in fifty. And it made the whole effort worthwhile. My heart wanted to sing. I quickly piled everything else on the kitchen desk and reached for the letter opener.

I'm never disappointed in this type of handwritten message that appears in the mailbox. It's the best, a treasure hidden among the throng of throw-aways. So rare is it now that when I see one of these wonderful envelopes, penned in familiar or unfamiliar script, my mind immediately begins searching the memory bank for reasons I would be getting a thank-you note or a written invitation.

I was delighted to discover it was neither, just a newsy note from a friend. Her notes are filled into the margins with what she'd planted in the garden, the varieties of birds that have graced her feeders in the past few days, what she has baked, and her volunteer activities. "The hummingbirds have finally arrived," she wrote. ". . . They are vying already with the bees for places at the feeders. . . . And it's so amusing to see the Baltimore orioles with their curved beaks land on the tiny hummingbird perches and try to drink . . ." We rarely talk on the telephone or e-mail each other. Nor do we fax. This is how we keep up with each other, and it is a true delight.

A Note of Encouragement

I ONCE KNEW A YOUNG WOMAN whose mental illness required that she be hospitalized for several years. Doctors remained baffled as to how to treat her. Then she was given pen and paper, and she began to write herself well, line after line, from the depths of the darkness of her troubled mind to the light of a whole, well one. It was amazing to read her poetry.

The healing art of writing—connecting our outer person and our inner self—has been practiced by many who have discovered that this is the path to personal wellness, inner development, and self-discovery.

The power to help heal and cheer others through what we write has been practiced since the dawn of civilized time. *Civilized time.* There is undoubtedly a connection between those who practice journaling and those who share words of encouragement with others.

And sometimes *we* need the words of encouragement. Don't be afraid to ask. "I'm feeling down today," an elderly relative wrote recently. "The new medication isn't working, and I had such hope this was going to solve the problem . . ." There's a myth out there that we should write *only* if we have a brilliant and glowingly happy bit of news to share. Not true.

But whenever possible, use your cheerful muscle to right your mood before you write your notes. When you do, bad news will take on a much more objective tone, and you will undoubtedly feel better about it, too.

Staying in Touch

A WISE WOMAN ONCE TOLD ME, "If you want to receive mail, you need to write." It's like a heartbeat, the keeping in touch with those you seldom see, but who are part of your past, present, and future. All relationships need nurturing with some sort of rhythm.

> *Dear Marinda,*
>
> *I love thinking back to the wonderful long weekend we spent in Carmel. Although it's very hard to imagine having an unpleasant time in such a beautiful setting, sharing it with you made it a "Top Ten Memory." I look at those pictures every few days and enjoy the warm glow of that weekend.*
>
> *Next quarter how about doing four days in San Francisco?*
>
> *I'm enclosing a few ideas I took from a Web site.*

I have a number of very special friends with whom I share ideas mainly through correspondence. It's a very curious and interesting fact that these ideas are best handwritten in notes. This practice, we've found, allows the writer and the recipient time to form a concept and to properly reflect on it. These notes have offered a huge source of inspiration and clarity. And discovery. They are on no particular schedule, but they arrive rather routinely. These discovery notes supercede even those rare and wonderful conversations when I feel wholly in sync with another soul. It's a unique way in which we discover something between us that neither might arrive at on her own.

Words written down take on an added weight and provide an invitation to ponder:

> *Dear Joan,*
>
> *. . . I found that to effect forgiveness I needed to have the apology first. It released me to say, "Yes, I forgive you."*
>
> *I know at times I'm able to forgive without someone first apologizing. What, do you think, makes the difference? . . .*

Many scholars and theologians report the value of such exploration and discovery communications.

Give an Extra Hooray

SOME OF THE CYCLES in life are greatly enriched when others join in to add wishes, written applause, and encouragement. Think about sending an additional note a few weeks after a big event when there can be a vacuum as the new life stage settles into a quiet pace. This is an ideal time to write a follow-up greeting that will probably stand alone, and mean even more. Here's one sent six months after a retirement:

> *Dear Alex,*
>
> *I wanted to drop a note at this stage after you have had a chance to exhaust your initial list of things you wanted to do after retirement to tell you, again, just how much you were appreciated here at Mayers.*

Now that your retirement "initiation" period is over, I hope golf and fishing are great sources of joy for you. (Thanks for the note with the picture of the rainbow trout.)

Remember that list of volunteer activities you requested? Well, here are the ones I thought you might be interested in, with the names of other Mayers retirees who are now involved. Contact any of them at their numbers listed.

Don't forget the retirees' dinner on the 15th. See you then, and I can't wait to hear your Alaskan fish story and your six-month report.

Bond Building

I KNOW SEVERAL WOMEN who have taken a new member of an association under their wing. One who lives in an East Coast city has "adopted" a "newbie" on the West Coast, and offers advice she thinks the new member will value. "Big Sisters" often find that an occasional note is a great benefit to a girl trying to find her way through the dicey waters of early teenhood. One recently wrote to her young friend:

Dear Melly,

I know this is going to be a very tough week for you with finals. I'm thinking about you every day. I have the schedule you gave me, and I'm sending up some special thoughts when I know you're taking one of your tests.

Remember how we did the review, and what we decided was the best way to spend the last two hours before a test.

I'm sure you'll do well. You had the history down cold.

Established Sunday school class members can also befriend guests and new members to the class through notes. One recently wrote,

"Cindy, How nice to have you in class today. I enjoy your contribution to the discussion, and I agree with you about contemplative prayer . . ."

Mothers- and daughters-in-law have found that sending regular, occasional notes, often with a small gift enclosed, is the best way to say—without saying it—I'm extending myself to form and cement a bond with you. Welcome to a unique sisterhood, a family where we are committed to always support each other. Know that I am here for you in a way that others are not. We have a bond, and it's growing. One mother-in-law wrote: "Krissie, Here are several springs of rosemary I just picked from my bush along with the recipe for rosemary chicken. It's the one Rafe used to like best . . ."

Include a little "relationship builder" in such notes. Enclose family "secret" recipes, those especially appreciated by the new spouse. A mother of two sons created the "McEaters Family Recipes," using three-ring binder notebooks, one for each of her daughters-in-law, then periodically sent them each family recipes written on appropriately sized paper to put in the notebooks. Her daughters-in-law, and her sons as well, reciprocated with a few of their spouse's "new favorites."

The relationship can deepen when it becomes one experienced Mom to a new Mom. One mother-in-law became a kind of mentor to the breastfeeding mother, sending a note of encouragement each month to the younger woman. When the infant turned six months old, she wrote: "This is my very favorite age! Randal will be able to laugh out loud, smile, and coo, but won't be able to get into anything! It's wonderful . . ."

Triathlete and "extreme sports" friends are also big on bond-building. They use periodic notes for keeping in touch, encouraging each other, comparing training techniques, and "sounding out" new theories. They also have developed a wonderful "love box" that they send back and forth to each other on special occasions. One athlete wrote about receiving her first box, "It was delivered to me as I crossed the finish line of an extreme sports event. I've never been so dirty, or so exhausted. Can you imagine my delight when I realized it contained my favorite soap, perfume, tea, and refreshing cream? Never was anything so welcome . . ."

Reconnecting

IT'S MUCH EASIER TO DROP a note to someone you've neglected, maybe for a very long time, than it is to see them at a reunion after you'd promised to stay in contact. It's much better to write before you reconnect: "Well, my resolve to stay in touch didn't work as well as I'd planned, but I'm going to attend the reunion, and I hope you'll be there, and we'll get a little time to sit down and catch up again . . ." Then think of something you can do to keep the conversation going after the reunion.

Reconnecting on a very intermittent basis sometimes makes sense. I have a number of former colleagues with whom it works well. We may communicate with each other only at holiday time, unless we plan to meet up at a professional convention. Then I'll write: "Here we are again at convention time. I'm really hoping you'll be there this year. Can we get together for dinner and catch-up? . . ."

Writing to Kids

Tell me a fact and I'll learn. Tell me a truth and I'll believe. But tell me a story and it will live in my heart forever.

—INDIAN PROVERB

I'M ESPECIALLY FOND OF "story notes" to kids. They work very well for nieces, nephews, grandchildren, and friends' children with whom you want to continue to develop a loving connection. Send your own handmade postcards created by gluing a photo onto a 3" by 5" or 4" by 6" index card.

Keeping the story going often means asking a question the child can answer in a returning note or an ensuing conversation. Send them photos from trips, or even pictures of pets, or a reminder or fun shared. One grandma sent a photo of herself standing on a dock and wrote: "Cassie, What is this? Do you remember? You're right: This is the dock where we caught all those bass while you were here last summer, and from which Gramps went out in his belly boat. Wasn't he funny? Gramps thinks that by this summer you'll be big enough to try the small belly boat and flippers in the pond where we went fishing . . ."

An aunt wrote to her niece: "Camilla, I just ran across this photo of us camping. Remember this rock wall where we repelled? They've built a brand-new one (see the other photo), and are calling it 'the expert wall.' Think you can tackle it this summer? I'm putting in a copy of the sheet from the center so you can see if you qualify . . ."

18

Love Notes

... Great painters learned to paint by copying Old Masters in museums. You can learn to write by trying to copy the writers you like. Writing helps you to express your deepest feelings ...
—JACQUELINE KENNEDY ONASSIS, 1980

Memory will slip; a letter will keep.
—A WELSH PROVERB

LOVE NOTES ARE created to express how much you care. The very act of writing it down gives flow and form to what is in your heart. It makes your message more meaningful, both to you and to the one you love.

Why a *written* note? Think for a moment. Which would you rather receive to learn of someone's affection: a voice mail message, an e-mail, a typed missive, or a handwritten note? Of course the answer is a timeless, handwritten note.

Content, of course, is everything. Putting the *love* into the note is what gives it magic. I learned this lesson first hand while dating "The Shrink," for whom I cared a great deal. He would begin to talk about our future together, then would say: "What I really need to do is write something to you, and tell you just how I feel about *us*. It's too difficult to say. I do so much better when I have time to reflect and write it down. . . ."

Over a period of weeks my anticipation built to a roar in my heart, until one day after a lunch together he handed me a fat envelope and said, "Read this when you get home."

Of course I read it line by line, and several times over.

Never have I felt a more total disconnect. The five tightly written pages, handsomely scripted in clear and hardy penmanship, were filled with lament about his dog that had recently run away, and the discontent he felt with his career. While these were subjects I was very willing to discuss with him, they were hardly what I was expecting to find in a note I believed was going to be about *us*. In a note I believed was going to declare his affection for *me*. A love note this was *not*!

Focus

BY DEFINITION, a love note must be focused on the *love* of your life. He or she needs to be the main character to really make it work. This, of course, can take the form of your feelings for the person, and your hopes and dreams about your relationship.

Start by jotting down a few words or phrases in your notebook, based on those *W* words, to clarify your direction and ensure you're on track:

- *Who* is he or she?

- *What* do I most admire about him or her?

- *What* do I want to tell this person about me, about how I feel about him or her, about us?

- *Why* am I writing?

- *What* do I want him or her to do after reading my note?

Depending on what you write, you may also want to address the *when*, *where*, and *how much* questions.

Don't fall into the trap of my ex-friend, The Shrink. Don't make yourself the main character in your note, hoping that will help to build a bond with this person for whom you feel real affection.

> *She walks in beauty, like the night*
> *Of cloudless climes and starry skies;*
> *And all that's best of dark and bright*
> *Meet in her aspect and her eyes.*
>
> —LORD BYRON,
> *She Walks in Beauty*

> *Beauty is eternity gazing at itself in a mirror.*
> *But you are eternity and you are the mirror.*
>
> —KAHLIL GIBRAN,
> *The Prophet*

> *O lovely eyes of azure,*
> *Clear as the waters of a brook that run*
> *Limpid and laughing in the summer sun.*
>
> —HENRY WADSWORTH LONGFELLOW,
> *The Masque of Pandora*

Put yourself in the note only to reflect how wonderful the one you love is: "I see the twinkle in your blue, blue eyes, and it sends an electric, thrilling shock through me." "Your sense of humor rocks my world, you're a lovably funny, funny man." "I love the way you can walk into a room, and so quickly see what needs to be done, and in which order. You are masterful." "You are the most patient person I've ever met; I marvel at the sense of calm you wear in chaos."

Reflected Attractiveness

THERE IS, of course, the art of making the one you love the main character, *understood*, that is, as seen through your eyes: "I was, I now realize, a very morose and too-serious person before I met you; you are the light (and lite) of my life." "You've made a dramatic change in my life, and it's all for the better. I think you're simply great." "Once upon a time there was a person who spent all his daytime and most of his nighttime hours at the job, and he became a dull, dull, dull boy; that was before I met you—you've rearranged my priorities. And it has made me oh so happy."

> *How do I love thee?*
> *Let me count the ways.*
> *I love thee to the depth and breadth and height*
> *My soul can reach,*
> *when feeling out of sight*
> *For the ends of Being and ideal Grace.*
> —ELIZABETH BARRETT BROWNING,
> *Sonnets from the Portuguese*

And for serious, committed love, nothing is so sweet to your loved one as a note of commitment that makes *us*, and *our love*, the focus:

> *Drink to me only with thine eyes,*
> *And I will pledge with mine;*
> *Or leave a kiss but in the cup*
> *And I'll not look for wine.*
> —BEN JONSON
> *To Celia*

My true-love hath my heart, and I have his,
By just exchange one for another given:
I hold his dear, and mine he cannot miss,
There never was a better bargain driven:
My true love hath my heart, and I have his.

His heart in me keeps him and me in one,
My heart in him his thoughts and senses guides:
He loves my heart, for once it was his own,
I cherish his because in me it bides:
My true love hath my heart, and I have his.

—SIR PHILIP SIDNEY,
The Bargain

Let me not to the marriage of true minds
Admit impediments. Love is not love
Which alters when it alternation finds,
Or bends with the remover to remove:
O, no! it is an ever-fixed mark,
That looks on tempests and is never shaken;
It is the star to every wandering bark,
Whose worth's unknown, although his height be taken.
Love's not Time's fool, though rosy lips and cheeks
Within his bending sickle's compass come;
Love alters not with his brief hours and weeks,
But bears it out even to the edge of doom.
If this be error and upon me proved,
I never wrote, nor no man ever loved.

—WILLIAM SHAKESPEARE
Sonnet CXVI

Love bears all things, believes all things,
hopes all things, endures all things.

Love never fails. Where there are
prophecies, they will fail, where there are
tongues, they shall cease, where there is
knowledge, it shall vanish away.

For we know in part, and we prophesy in part,
but when that which is perfect comes,
the imperfect will go away.

When I was a child, I spoke like a child,
I understood as a child, I thought as a child,
but when I became a man,
I put away childish things.

For now we see through a glass dimly,
but then face to face. Now I know in
part, but then I shall know
even as I am known.

And now these three things abide,
faith, hope, and love,
but the greatest of these is love.
　　　　—1 Corinthians, Chapter 13, Verses 4–13

Looking for Inspiration

YOU ARE NOT, as you may sometimes think, hopelessly word-stumped in the romantic ideas department. There are many places for you to go for inspiration. First try the traditional ones: expose yourself to art, poetry, nature, and music. Then think about the person you want to write to, and begin to write. I suggest a little "Love Notebook" that can contain all such musings. You may return to it over and over for inspiration.

When you feel uncertain of how the other person feels about you, or of your own prowess as a wordsmith, use a quote from one of the masters. You don't even need to go too overboard in your reference. Try something like, "I've always loved Byron, especially this poem . . ." or, "It strikes me as a worthy goal, to know a love so pure as this . . ." Or, say nothing at all, just quote the poem and reference the poet. If you want to be more serious, try, "I think Byron had love like ours in mind when he wrote this . . . ," or "Longfellow has said, perfectly, what I want to say to you . . . ," "I can't improve on these words, but I do know it's what I feel. . . ."

Love with a Sense of Humor

YOU DON'T NEED TO BE totally serious. Sometimes it's fun to be light, and just a little silly. Often humor works well. It can be the wisest approach for a young relationship, a friendship, or a loved one who shies away from all things gooey. Try personalizing some old lines:

> *Roses are red,*
> *Violets are blue,*
> *I'm no poet,*
> *But I truly love you!*

> *Two roads diverged on a busy bus,*
> *Once we were two,*
> *But now we are us!*

Mirror, mirror on the wall,
I no longer have to ask Y'all,
Now I'm sure: Christine's
The fairest of them all!

Of all the people who write verse,
Perhaps I'm the very worse.
(See?)
No mind's eye do I hold for rhyme,
No winning sense of place or time.
I only know this to be true
I truly, wholly do love you.

Oh, the places we'll go now,
The things we will see.
Our love was so full
Now there'll be three!

But there's a thing I'd like to say,
And praises sing, all night and day.
They are to you, Dear One, you see,
You are everything, and most precious to me.

You get the idea. A silly, sweet, or even slightly off-kilter poem that expresses how you feel in simple rhyme and meter can really make it anywhere. Several years ago, I attended a very formal wedding ceremony where the couple declared the vows they'd written themselves. She said, "You are the topping on my Sunday, the ice cream in my à la mode." He said, "Your love is like a cool brook to my thirsty heart, like a high light beam to my dark highway." And they are living happily ever after!

Using Comparisons and Contrasts

USING BOTH METAPHORS AND similes is sure to endear you to the object of your desire. Use similes, two unlike words connected with "as" or "like," to draw a comparison: "pure as fresh-driven snow," "meek as a lamb," "soft as silk," "colorful as a rainbow," "eyes like stars," "a smile like sunshine," "cheeks like rose pedals," "sweet as honey," or "being with you is like wearing my favorite, fluffy slippers—cuddly, comfortable, safe, and at home."

Use a metaphor, a word or phrase that usually means one thing to mean something else, to make an implicit comparison: "your porcelain skin is flawless," "my heart, once an iceberg, is a white, hot fire," "you are a shining star in my dark, dreary life." Or try, "your love is a safe shelter, dry and warm against the cold;" or "you are my shade in a parched, dry land."

Measure for Measure

THE MISMATCHED LOVE NOTE, though it does everything right, is the note that won't bring the results you want. So don't save your "real" feelings just for the note. Be fairly sure of your feelings, as well as those of your intended, before you write. Still, it's far better to be rejected after the other person has read your note, and had an opportunity to reflect on what you have written, than it is to be expecting a response that doesn't come when you confess your love in a face-to-face meeting.

Talking on Paper

REMEMBER THAT YOU'LL want to sound like yourself in your note, so make your prose conversational. Most of us have both a formal and a more casual voice, and you'll want to sound just right for the words and impact you're trying for. If you're in doubt, read your note aloud to yourself and listen for the familiar words you use in conversation. Listen, too, to the tone and to rhythms that distinguish the way you'd really say the words. This may not sound like you: "Your unparalleled beauty," "your brilliance of mind," "your magnificent utterances." This may have a truer ring to your ear: "I know I've said this a thousand times, but I just wanted to write it down so you could read it anytime . . ."

Opening Your Heart

ONCE YOU GET STARTED, don't stop until the outpouring from your heart is complete. It's this *flow* that, once started, yields the best and fullest expression. Write in your notebook first, so you can do a little tuning-up here and there later. You'll find you've used the same word two or three times and want to substitute, or you'll rephrase, deleting a line or a sentence, or adding one, until it sounds purely like what you want to say.

Creating an Occasion

ADDING A SMALL GIFT to your message shows thoughtfulness and heart. Who wouldn't melt at the sign of pressed red rose petals and blue violet petals slipped inside a note that read as follows:

Roses are truly red
(you see)
Violets are blue
('tis true)
This petal bouquet
Means I'm so in love with you!

Imagine how impressed a wife of twenty years was to get a love note with the pressed flowers from a boutonniere she'd given her husband on the date of their very first formal dance!

Vary the intensity and even the style of your note. Sometimes make it hot, sometimes not. Sometimes light and fun, sometimes more serious.

An occasion can give your note completely new dimensions. Happy is the husband who opens his suitcase or briefcase on a business trip and finds a love note:

Gosh, I miss you already
before you're actually gone.
But it's only 78 hours and 8.5 minutes
until we'll be together again.
I'm planning a tiny surprise for your return.
Present this "Mystery Coupon"
at the door.
And be prepared to be surprised!

Or the wife who discovers this, pinned to the notes she has in her pocket for making an important board of directors presentation:

Just smile, and you'll
Knock em dead!
That's the effect

You always have on me.
You'll do great!
I love you.

You'll think of many ways to make little treasures, and pleasures, mean the world. Maybe a note on the bed pillow:

I didn't happen to have a mint,
but I have something very sweet in mind.
I love you!

A Circle of Love

DON'T LEAVE OTHERS OUT of the circle of your love. Children are tickled with notes in their lunch bag or backpack, on their bedroom door, hanging from the refrigerator, on their breakfast plate, in their gym bag, or tucked into their after-school snack.

Love Note "To Do" Lists

IF LOVE NOTES HAVE been missing from your life and the lives of those in your circle, set a goal of two per person per month. They can even be post-it notes on the mirror: "See who's the fairest of them all? You!" "These shoes are for jumping high, and that's exactly what you'll do today in your basketball game. That'll be Dad and me in the stands rooting for our very special star!" "Now the studying is done, and I'm sure you'll do very well! I love you. Mom." Make nonoccasions occasions; and make small occasions noteworthy:

What a joy to share with you—
this day when our "baby" goes off in the big, yellow
school bus for her first day of school.

I don't think I've ever loved you more,
or felt my love for you so deeply
as when I found you and Philippa
fast asleep in the rocking chair.

The real secret to wonderful love notes is just to open up your heart and let the words pour out. They are all in there. The marvelous principle of love shared is that it becomes love multiplied. Share it lavishly!

PART THREE

Notes of Sorrow and Sympathy

19

Illness and Accidents

. . . I was sick, and ye visited me.
—MATTHEW 25:35

LIFE OFFERS TOO FEW OPPORTUNITIES to share our true humanity with another person. There's no better time than when someone you know is sidelined due to an illness, injury, surgery, or even an "elective procedure." Your personal note can make a cheering connection. It can even promote healing.

The first and vital point in preparing to write a message at this time is to *tune into who the person is, the reason for her timeout, and—as precisely as possible—how she feels about what has happened.* Use all this information to give you writing cues. Then factor into your message an upbeat reference to something you two have in common, and be sensitive to her prognosis. Sound difficult? It's not; you can easily do it with just a little heart. Start by jotting down a few points.

To Whom Should You Write?

WHILE YOUR MESSAGE SHOULDN'T go beyond the boundaries of your relationship, or superimpose your beliefs on someone else, don't assume it won't be welcome. An atheist friend of mine who had just gotten very bad news about her illness quickly responded when I asked if she would be offended to know she is in my prayers. "No. I'm open to all the prayers and good thoughts I can get."

What Should You Say?

YOUR MESSAGE JUST NEEDS to say, you're not alone. I'm here. I know you are suffering, and I care.

Refer generally to what has happened. Not doing so can make you appear calloused or uncaring:

I was very sorry to hear about your accident. . . .

Karen mentioned you are in the hospital. I'm hoping that it's just a minor tune-up, and that your recovery will be swift and complete. . . .

I'm sure you'll be better than ever once you're healed. Bo Jackson and many others have found hip replacements got them off the sidelines and back into the action. I'm hoping for a wonderful outcome for you, too . . .

I'm hoping with each day you're "more better" than the day before . . .

Being in the hospital certainly isn't fun, but I'm hoping this surgery will finally do the trick . . .

When you haven't heard details of the problem from the person directly, don't go into specifics. It's important to remember that the patient may *not* want others to know the details of what has happened. An employee suffered a heart attack, and I was told that he feared this fact could make him unemployable. I certainly didn't mention the reason for his hospitalization in my card. Take your cues only from the patient or the person closest to him or her.

And don't offer up something like, "I *know exactly how you feel*," or "*I had something like this*," or negative comparative statements like, "*Ritchie's father had these symptoms before he was diagnosed . . .*" These statements aren't helpful, and they don't promote the empathy you may intend.

Tuning In

SOMETIMES, IN OUR EAGERNESS to help, we forget several basic things: being a patient and feeling vulnerable doesn't mean a person wants to be treated like she's incapable of making her own decisions; she may want what has happened treated confidentially; she may not want to be fussed over. Remember, it's not your job to make the patient feel better. You may not be able to do that. But don't make her feel worse by intruding.

When I was hired to substitute for the managing editor of a magazine while she was recovering from a surgery, I was told, "she eats, sleeps, and breathes this job." The editor, herself, did not mention anything about her medical situation. In fact, she avoided talking about it. She'd told only two of her closest colleagues that she was going to be "gone for four weeks."

I was uncertain what kind of message to send her; but I was very sure she would *not* welcome any reference to her surgery. Nor, I was certain, would she want a hospital visit, or one of those greeting cards that had been circulated around the office for everyone to write a little message on and sign—at least not initiated by me, an outsider.

I sent by delivery service a simple message with a potted plant based on our *work connection*—temporary as it was:

Greta,

Hopefully, today is a better day than yesterday, and you're one day closer to feeling completely well again.

My "acting manager" skills can't substitute for the creative and masterful way you perform this job, but you have left me wonderful instructions, and I promise to continue to try hard to follow them exactly, and not to get things into a muddle before you return. The next issue is now put together and will be out on time.

It's evident that you're greatly missed here. Both Rita and Laura have been very helpful, but I see the glimmer of hope in their eyes when someone mentions your return.

Here at the office, many have offered to get you anything you'd like while convalescing. Jan asked this morning. I, too, would be happy to arrange to have anything you'd like delivered to you. Just call me.

This new rosebush for your rose garden was named "Recovery," and that's my sincere wish for you.

Is It Serious?

YOUR MESSAGE NEEDS TO REFLECT the measure of the illness or injury. Keeping it light works when you know the person well, and the outcome will be good; but it's not a good choice for a very serious situation, or when you don't know the patient well.

For the person who had a hammertoe "unhammered," as a friend of mine just did, writing a message wasn't difficult:

Ricki,

I can hardly wait to see how this improves your serve and volley game; after all, I have a vested interest. I'm waiting eagerly to see the new speed of my doubles partner: you'll be at the net in three strides now!

While you're propping that foot up, I thought you might have time to study the doubles strategies in this book. Then you can teach me. You know I instruct easily: all you have to do is yell, "Mine."

Sending a message of comfort to a new friend who quickly became very ill was quite a different matter. Complications after her rather routine surgery left the doctors mystified. Within a few days, an insidious infection had begun that couldn't be identified or eliminated, and she became gravely ill.

While I hadn't known her a long time, I considered her a very special friend, one with whom I had a strong connection. I quickly did a little homework and asked her husband if she shared a love for one of my favorite poets. He said he thought she did. (He was giving daily e-mail updates to a group of us about her condition, and we were sending return e-mails of encouragement, which he read to her each day.) I had also talked with her on the telephone. But, of course, these communications don't substitute for a personal, heartfelt, handwritten message.

I knew my friend is a devout Catholic, and I also knew from the e-mail messages and from talking with her that time, anxiety, fear, and the boredom of lying in the hospital were all weighing heavily on her. (She was in isolation and not allowed visitors.) A book of poetry was something her husband could read to her, I reasoned, and the poems themselves were inspiring and comforting.

My note was delivered to the ICU unit along with the book and a potted orchid, which had to remain at the nurse's station. The note read:

Jennifer,

I'm hoping that today will be the day the doctors find the right antibiotic to kill off this infection. I'm praying that it is.

While I was thinking about you, I thought of this book of poems, especially the beauty of the faces of faith and hope described in the poem on page 73. I'm sure it will become one of your favorites in the book, if it isn't already. Colin said he'd like to read it to you. It describes, too, the strong faith in God I've witnessed and know is yours.

Before the blooms on this orchid fade, I hope to see you back on the dance floor at The Cotillion demonstrating the latest tango move you've mastered. Remember, the next ball is June 4. It would be fabulous to see you there.

I've asked Colin if there's anything I can deliver to you— books on tape, music on disk or tape, library books, or real food. Please tell him if there is, or call me, and I'll get what you'd like and bring it to the nursing station.

Please know you are in my thoughts and prayers every hour of every day. I'm sending along all my wishes for a miraculous and speedy recovery.

The get well wishes can also come from a group:

Dear Noodles,

We were so sorry to hear about your nasty spill. When Booker said conditions were extremely poor, and "Noodles reported that, but she wouldn't penalize the team by refusing to ski," Rennie and I both said, "That sounds like Noodles."

The team got together and created a new five-pointed star award for the most-admired girl on the ski team, in the ER, and in the OR. You took First Place! Please wear it with pride (celebration banquet and official speeches as soon as you're up and around).

Now, Champ, how about letting some of your teammates pick up the slack? Will you let me take over teaching your Monday night class, and could Malcolm spot for you at the animal rescue center until your leg is completely healed?

We've got a relay car pool organized for your transportation to rehab, and for whenever you need something. Just call the person on the "Patrol Duty List." The same goes for "Rehab Partnering" (the second list).

We all salute you. Please consider using these dedicated team members to help. We all want to see you back in winning form, in the lineup, and on the slopes next year.

Connecting the Dots

USE WHAT YOU HAVE in common, and the people you both know, as sources to relieve the anxiety and stress over things other than getting well. Connecting with others diminishes the loneliness and isolation. Galvanize those who can help, but be sure not to take over or act in any way that could feel intrusive. The patient is the same person she was, and having one more thing out of her control could add to her feeling of helplessness. Unless she prefers that you take over, try something like this:

Andrea is willing to fill in on the Philips project for you until you're able to get back to the office. Will that work?

The bridge club volunteers to bring over meals for the month. (Your entire family may beg never to see another casserole after June 1.) I'll call Jim to get your instructions about when to arrange dinner time. . . .

What a smart girl you are, having two of the best physical therapists in town as best friends. We're ready when you are if you'd allow us to help you rehab . . .

We've postponed the tournament for a month so you can participate if you'd like to . . .

Timing and Visits

WITH THE ARRIVAL of conveyor-belt "day" surgery, most people aren't in the hospital long enough to wrinkle the sheets. Even very serious surgeries command only a few inpatient days, so you need to check and use precision timing to get flowers or other gifts delivered to the hospital. The hospital gift shop, services available through the Internet, local florists and other businesses, or even delivery services will make sure your gift and message get there. But while you're checking, ask the person closest to the patient if there are already too many flowers. It's often better to have them delivered to the patient after she gets home. This saves transporting them, too.

If you know the patient well, put some legs on your good wishes and visit—after first calling to make sure it's a good idea and a good time. Take something that will cheer. In hospitals, the food usually doesn't get five stars, so ask the patient what would taste good, and pick it up on the way, with something for yourself, too. The noises in hospitals are such that soothing music played through a headset might be welcome, or books on tape, or a disk. Or take a book of light fare.

When Things Don't Get Better

EVERY ILLNESS, accident, or surgery leaves the patient feeling some measure of vulnerability and experiencing some or all of the stages of grieving: denial, numbness, pain, sadness, depression, anxiety, isolation, and loss. You can succor the sick, ailing, injured, or heartsick with *periodic messages* that reassure the person she isn't alone in her time of trouble. When the prognosis is grim, your messages can be a great comfort, especially if you send them regularly and offer words of care and solace.

When a young husband was dying of a brain tumor, many friends sent written messages that stated what he'd meant to their lives. Late one afternoon, while reading messages to him, his wife asked, "Do you want me to stop? Is this bothering you?" He answered, "No, it's very gratifying."

You can start with something like:

I'm hoping this will be a better day . . .

I haven't told you nearly often enough how much you mean to me . . .

You are constantly in my thoughts and prayers. May I tell you how important you are to me? . . .

I'm sending good thoughts today. . . . Remember the day. . . .

*. . . Our ice cream flavor for this week will be "Pecan Delight."
I'm coming, as usual, on Thursday, unless you need to re-
schedule. . . .*

*. . . This week's memory picture clue is: the year was 1984, the
place was New York City. Who are these people, and what was the
event?*

*. . . I hope you're feeling up for negotiations today, because here's
the baseball card I'll trade you for your . . .*

*. . . The enclosed stamps for your collection should finish your
states series. . . .*

The following are excerpts from notes recorded in *Ghost Soldiers*
by Sides Hampton. These notes were sent in thanks for help offered
prisoners in Cabanatuan, a World War II Japanese prison camp near
Manila.

Dear Friend,

   *So you are Phil's wife. Your letter was a God-send. I had
begun to think that we in here were the Forgotten Men. Thanks
for the money. I sure can use it. . . .*

Hello High Pockets:

   *When I got your letter I came to life again. Gee, it's good to
know someone like you. You deserve more gold medals than all of
us in here together. You've done more for the boys' morale in here
than you'll ever know . . .*

   *. . . We read the letter you wrote Yeager all over the hospital
area and everyone got a big laugh. It sure cheered the men up. . . .*

Kids' Greetings

IT'S ESPECIALLY heart-rending when kids get sick or injured. Any diversionary greetings you send—especially with a small game or activity—can be golden. And it will be appreciated by the whole family. Make it cheerful, colorful, and fun.

You may not have the artistic skill of Beatrix Potter, but you can write a little verse if you start out with something like:

> *Roses are red, Violets are Blue, and at this moment—I'm oh, so sorry to say—so are You. But not for long . . .*

> *Oh, the Places We'll Go, the Things We Will See,*
> *When You're Cast is Off, And You Travel with Me!!*
> *I'm thinking a celebration trip to the zoo*
> *Is the very thing that will get your leg really working again . . .*

> *I'm so sorry to hear, my special dear, that you're sick. Now here's a rhyme I hope will cheer: There once was a Blue lagoon, a purple moon, and a red baboon. How many other words can you find that rhyme, besides* spoon? *Write them on this note I've enclosed, stuff it inside the stamped envelope, and send it to me. If you come up with more than twelve new ones, it's lunch at noon! The two of us, and we'll have chocolate sundaes with a big spoon, and buy a red balloon. (Oh, how many is that?) . . .*

You can always tell a story: "Once upon a time, there was a wonderful, stupendous, nearly-as-tall-as-the-countertop, seven-year-old girl who was, incidentally, loved very much. She had golden hair that came down to her waist—almost. She was in the second grade and doing very, very well. Until she fell. Ouch! . . ." Or, "Once upon a time, a little boy I love very much got an unfriendly germ. . . ." Children love stories in which they are the main characters; they especially love them if they are the heroes.

Include in your message some validating themes, like it's okay to cry and feel sad, to be restless, and to be upset: ". . . And when she fell, she really, really fell. Something in her arm—which is where she fell—went pop. It broke, that tiny bone right down by the end where her hand is. It hurt and hurt. And she cried. . . ." Or, ". . . 'This bad germ,' the doctor said, 'we'll just have to get rid of it, and we'll fig-ure out how. It's going to take some shots and some medicine.' Who likes shots? 'I don't' said the boy's dad. 'They hurt,' said the boy's mom. 'I can't look,' said the boy's Aunt Pam. . . ."

End with hope and good cheer: ". . . The end of this story isn't written yet, but it's going to have some very wonderful things hap-pen, like the girl playing soccer this summer with her new, strong, better-than-ever arm. . . ." Or, ". . . The good thing about bad germs that are all gone is that little boys, like this one named Eli, get to do very special things, like take a trip to . . ."

Try your hand at festooning your message with a few drawings, smiling faces, Xs and Os, and big, red-colored lipstick kisses. Stick in some cheery things, like decal "tattoos" for a cast, pictures of the future that include something the child can look forward to doing, or photos of your last outing together. You can even draw some little Beatrix Potter-like characters for your story. Enclose paper and a stamped, self-addressed envelope, and suggest, "Maybe you can draw a mouse that looks better than mine. Will you draw me one on this paper, tell me his name, and ask your Mom to put your drawing in the mail?"

Or, if you're not comfortable with the storyteller role, tell a real-life, encouraging tale. ". . . I remember when I was seven and broke my leg. I cried a lot at first. But pretty soon I was hobbling around, and hopping up and down the stairs on my good foot. Your mother called me, 'Hop-Along,' and teased me, saying it would make me topsy-turvy for the rest of my natural life. And she still, sometimes, says that it has. And she still calls me 'Topsy.'"

To build in some when-you're-well anticipation, try a plan for the future: ". . . Here's what I suggest. As soon as your fever has been gone for three days, and all the pox have lost their scabs, you give me a call. We'll either go to Stubby's or Jack's. Afterwards, we can go to the baseball game. What do you think? Your doctor said I could circle this game on the calendar: May 19. 'I'm sure,' he said, 'Bobbi will be ready by then.' So, here's your copy of the calendar. Mark off the days . . ." Or, "I'm thinking a very special girl, who is recovered from her surgery, should have a nearly grown-up lunch with her Auntie Fritz at the Brown Palace. I'm also thinking that July 15 would be a perfect day for it. . . ."

Make it a joint message. If you're a teacher, den mother, coach, scout leader, after-school counselor, or parent, include little messages from others with an update on something that will keep the child in touch. "Now our record is four and seven, and we need you back in the line-up. All the team members have included messages. . . ." "You'll still have enough time to get your project finished. We've saved enough red paint for your car. . . ."

You can build a real connection if you become a serial note sender to a child who will need a while to recuperate. Try something like, "Can you guess what I have in mind for a puzzler for next week? Bet you can't."

Here are some other ideas for something to include to make a get-all-better-soon care package: a deck of cards like Authors, Fish, or one of the many others available; or slip in a couple of collector baseball or other sports cards into the envelope. A balloon for a small child, a book of paper dolls, a coloring book, an activities book, a video game, or a word book might be the perfect thing for breaking the monotony of being bedridden. A small airplane or toy, or anything that can be assembled and played with on a bed tray, will also be appreciated.

Here are three letters from Beatrix Potter to young friends from *Letters to Children from Beatrix Potter*, collected and introduced by Judy Taylor:

March 8th 95   *2, Bolton Gardens*
                                                                                      London, S.W.

My dear Noel,

I am so sorry to hear through your Aunt Rosie that you are ill, you must be like this little mouse, and this is the doctor Mr Mole, and Nurse Mouse with a tea-cup. I hope the little mouse will soon be able to sit up in a chair by the fire.

I went to the zoo on Wednesday & saw the new giraffe. It is a young one, very pretty, and the keeper says it will grow a good deal taller. . . .

                                                                         I remain yrs aff
                                                                         Beatrix Potter

Christmas 1901
My dear Freda,

Because you are fond of fairy-tales and have been ill, I have made you a story all for yourself—a new one that nobody has read before.

And the queerest thing about it—is that I heard it in Gloucestershire, and it is true! at least about the tailor, the waistcoat, and the 'No more twist'.

There ought to be more pictures towards the end, and they would have been the best ones; only Miss Potter was tired of it! Which was lazy of Miss Potter.

                                                                                           yrs aff
                                                                                           H.B.P.

Mrs. Rebeccah
  Puddleduck,
Farm Yard.
Dear Beccy,
   *I am sorry to hear of your sore throat, but what can you expect
if you will stand on your head in a pond? I will bring the flannel
petticoat & some more head drops directly.*

yr. sincere friend,
Ribby

20

Divorce

Divorce is the psychological equivalent of a triple coronary bypass. After such a monumental assault on the heart, it takes years to amend all the habits and attitudes that led up to it.

—MARY KAY BLAKELY

THERE'S NO ONE TO mourn over and bury, no natural, physical object of your grieving when there's a divorce. And there may be all those attending ugly emotions that can cloud the clearest eye: anger, humiliation, sense of loss, and a crushing blow to your sense of self-worth.

The divorced person left behind when a partner leaves may even feel like a friend of mine who wailed, "In the divorce settlement he even got the friends!" Isolation can feel complete, and even in our post-modern society—with divorce half as common as marriage—we struggle with how to negotiate such turbulent waters. It's difficult for the divorcing partners, and it's difficult for family, friends, and colleagues.

When one partner is left feeling crushed like an unsuspecting bug, the reflex is to enter a cocoon and hide. "Let me just roll up here and die," a friend sobbed. She added, "I can't face the firing squad of social opinion, see the looks, endure the turned heads, or hear the whispers." She especially dreaded seeing anyone to whom she might feel compelled to say, "He has met someone else, has fallen in love, has left, and we are divorcing." And she wondered if, perhaps, she was the last to learn of it. (She was.) It would have been easier, another friend cried, "to have signed up for a public flogging."

Friends sometimes avoid divorcing friends if they see them in public because they, too, don't know what to say. "I wanted to comfort her, to somehow make it easier," one friend told me. "But I didn't know if she wanted to talk about it. I didn't know what to say."

Why Write?

IT'S NOT COWARDLY—whether you are a friend, relative, colleague, or the person divorcing—to send a handwritten note at a time like this. It can, in fact, be especially helpful, merciful, and even therapeutic. "My biggest fear was that I would break down and dissolve in tears," a friend said of her decision to inform her friends with a note instead of telephoning or telling them face to face. "And I must tell you it was very therapeutic, too. For those who responded with a note, it was so much easier to see them in person afterward. The stage had been set to discuss it, or not."

Exercising her pen, another friend said, and exercising her body to relieve the stress, were the best things she did to start to recover. "I tried, too, to keep essential things the same. While a number of people told me I wouldn't be myself for a while—a year—I tried very hard to be myself, to save my energy for all those vital decisions that had to be made, and to shield my children from as much of the pain and chaos as possible."

Delivering News

TELL ONLY THOSE PEOPLE to whom it makes a difference, initially, just those who need to know. This list may include your parents or other close relatives, close friends, employers, and landlord. (You will also need to send written notices and legal information to creditors, banks, credit card companies, and so forth, as your lawyer advises.) Prioritize and start with those relatives, like your parents, who will feel particularly aggrieved to learn it; and who will be embarrassed or offended to hear it from others before they hear it from you. Decide who you need to talk with, and to whom you will write.

You can make a handwritten announcement, which will save any number of public confessions. *Don't send out a printed announcement.* Start with a simple statement of fact:

I wanted you to hear this from me first: Richard and I are divorcing.

Sadly, Grace and I are beginning divorce proceedings.

Regrettably, David and I are divorcing.

I'm sorry to have to inform you that Jenny and I are divorced. We signed the final papers Friday.

I thought I should tell you that Jack and I are beginning divorce proceedings.

"No one," a divorce lawyer once told me, "can go to the bank and deposit a single ounce of satisfaction." That goes double for revenge.

As difficult as it may be, staunch the impulse to get even or strike a retaliatory blow, especially in writing. Instead, resolve to conduct yourself in a way you will never regret. Less is far better than more in your note; avoid all those grim details. If you need to write them down, do so, then read the note to yourself. Read it aloud—*only* to to yourself. Then tear it into tiny, tiny pieces and throw it away.

Need-to-Know Information

YOU ARE NOT OBLIGED to explain what happened, or to give any details. You may just need to let relatives, friends, and business associates know of a change of address, where you, your former partner, and the children will be receiving mail and communications:

> *The children and I will be staying in the house, and Darcie may, at least temporarily, be reached at 540 Temple Avenue.*

> *Please direct your communications to me to: 322 Madison Boulevard.*

> *My temporary address for the next six months is at my parents, 75 Sherman Street, Detroit, MI 49854. I will be remaining at Guilders, and may also be reached there. Mark will be taking a position in Los Angeles, and I'm sure he'll be in contact with you.*

A Personal Statement

YOU MAY WANT TO give reassurance about yourself, allay some fears, add a sentence or two of regret, or further set the stage for your next communication:

I'm sure you can appreciate how difficult things are at this time.
I'm simply not able to share any details at the moment. Perhaps I
never will be. It will be nice to see you at the convention. I look
forward to keeping some things "normal" in my life . . .

I know you always remained hopeful that we would be able to
resolve our differences. Unfortunately, we weren't, and while I've
so appreciated your support, this decision is now final . . .

I've appreciated your willingness to listen, and your continued
support through all this, and hope you don't feel your efforts went
unappreciated . . .

Closings

CLOSE WITH HOPE FOR the future and for a continuation of
your relationship, if that is appropriate:

I hope we will be able to maintain our friendship, although I
realize you were Miriam's friend before we met. . . .

Thank you for all your support. I do hope it will continue. . . .

The children are doing quite well, all things considered. I do trust
our next communication will contain much happier news.

I realize this is very difficult for you, and you didn't divorce any-
one. You are still Granna and Gramps to the children, and a very
special friend to me. I sincerely hope these things will not change,
even as so much else will. I'm committed to working very hard to
nurture our relationship, always . . .

Although we will no longer be related by marriage, it is my hope that we will be bound by the friendship we have developed over the years, and that we will continue to see a great deal of each other. . . .

Writing in Response

IT'S MOST IMPORTANT, if you love both partners, not to take sides. Be sure your tone remains nonjudgmental, neutral, and shows continuing support. A few other cautions: don't ask for details; don't be a conduit for gossip or even valid information about the former spouse; try to treat the ex-partners equally if you are friends of both; and volunteer to help, especially with the children, if you can. If children are treated the same by you, a relative or family friend, it will ease this difficult transition.

Your note needn't be long. Make a statement of sympathy; confirm or reaffirm your understanding of the former spouse's wishes about discussing the divorce, if appropriate; show continuing support; offer to help, if appropriate (be realistic, and be specific about what you are willing to do); and close with a hopeful sentence. If your note is to a colleague, write it essentially the same.

Opening Sentences

STATE THE REASON FOR your note immediately, and as tenderly as possible:

How very sorry I am to hear that Mary has filed for divorce. . . .

Please accept my heartfelt sympathies at this difficult time. . . .

This is very sad news, indeed, and I feel terrible for you. . . .

I'm profoundly sorry to hear you and James have decided to file for divorce. . . .

Divorce under any circumstances is extremely difficult, and I'm so sorry to hear of yours. . . .

What a difficult time for you. Randolph tells me your divorce is now final. Please accept my sympathies for the harrowing experience this must have been . . .

Cover Any Business

YOU MAY WANT TO respond to something stated in your friend's note of announcement, offer help, or add a sentence or two of commiseration:

There really aren't words at a time like this, when you are suffering, to express how badly I feel for you. I believe you invested the same abundance of love and care in your marriage that you do in every aspect of your life, and I know you have no basis to feel that you have failed. . . .

I would like to have Timmy over on Friday nights, just as we have in the past, and I wonder if you'll let me substitute for you in the car pool for the month of September. . . .

I'm sorry you and the girls are having to go through such a painful process. Please know that I am here, and can arrange to pick Cassie up from the new school and bring her home with

Julia and me until 6:30 P.M. each school night for the six weeks until you move. . . .

I know making this decision has been ever so difficult, and I know you didn't make it without first trying every avenue of possible reconciliation. Do not blame yourself, and don't give up your dreams for a wonderful future. . . .

Although I haven't gone through a divorce, I've seen the suffering of my sister and niece and nephew, and I would only encourage you not to entertain thoughts that you have failed. You have not. There's a much brighter tomorrow for you, I'm sure of it. . . .

Closings

CLOSE WITH A POSITIVE thought, and one of hope for the future:

You are in my thoughts each day, and I look forward to a bright future for you, and with you.

I stand by your decision, and offer you my support in the weeks ahead. If you'd like, I suggest late afternoon chats (about four o'clock). Feel free to call. I remember that was the toughest time of the day for me. I'm thinking positive thoughts for you, Jen. I know what a wonderful person you are, and I believe there's much happiness in your future.

The extent of your suffering indicates to me just how much effort you made to make your marriage work. The added injustice here *would be if you continue to blame yourself. You deserve every happiness, and I know something very special awaits you.*

Some say healing is mostly about time, and my hope is that you are kind to yourself and give yourself that gift. You are a wonderful and worthy person, and in the not-very-distant future your friends will help you reaffirm that about yourself.

Writing to me couldn't have been easy, and I admire you for all the strength you've shown through this whole ordeal. There are only better days ahead, and many, many wonderful new things you haven't yet even dreamed about.

Yes, this is the end of something that was very dear, and I grieve with you. But it is also the beginning of something; and I know for sure that there are wonderful things ahead for you.

21

Condolences

Can I see another's woe
And not be in sorrow too?
Can I see another's grief,
And not seek for kind relief?

— WILLIAM BLAKE

The distance that the dead have gone
Does not at first appear
Their coming back seems possible
For many an ardent year.

— EMILY DICKINSON

. . . look in thy
heart and write.
— ASTROPHEL AND STELLA (1591)

NO ONE IS GOOD at handling death. Some are just more practiced. The most important thing to remember is that the death of a
loved one is a uniquely private grief; no one grieves quite like another.
I have a friend who at fifty-one lost her eighty-seven-year-old
mother. She cried secretly and inconsolably for well over a year, then
confided one day in desperation. "No one understands." My husband said, 'Isn't it time you just got over it?' And I don't understand
it myself. I just feel so sad, and so alone in the world."

There is no formula. Grief is not linear; it has no timetable. It has
a beginning, but no predictable end.

Why Should We Write?

WHEN SOMEONE DIES WE have the opportunity to demonstrate the very best of our humanity—to offer solace at life's most difficult moments. It's also an opportunity to celebrate the life of the person now gone. These are very good reasons to write.

"Every man's death diminishes me; no man is an island," John Donne said.

Writing will strengthen your connection with the griefstricken by offering comfort. It will also demonstrate your support, and help you mourn your own loss.

It is important to remember that grief wears many faces: denial and isolation, anger, bargaining, depression, and, hopefully and eventually, acceptance. Your handwritten note can help the grieving at any of these stages, but it will be the most comforting during the last two. This is the reason we should write more than once.

The young widow whose husband died suddenly of a brain tumor said, "I wouldn't have been able to make it without the continuing messages of family and friends, and their help. Especially difficult are the special times, like the birthdays of the children, that we used to celebrate together. And the anniversary of his death."

"I was afraid Derek would be forgotten," another young widow said. "Reading the written notes helped assuage my fears."

Grief Among Strangers

EVEN IF WE DON'T know the deceased well, we can write. Our relationship to the person we are writing to should, however, guide us. Whenever possible, take your cues from the grieving person, and stay within the boundaries of your relationship with her or him.

When President Abraham Lincoln wrote to Mrs. Lydia Bixby, who lost five sons fighting for the Union in the Civil War, he demonstrated the restraint of a stranger:

> *Dear Madam:*
>
> *I have been shown in the files of the War Department a statement of the Adjutant General of Massachusetts that you are the mother of five sons who have died gloriously on the field of battle. I feel how weak and fruitless must be any word of mine which should attempt to beguile you from the grief of a loss so overwhelming. But I cannot refrain from tendering you the consolation that may be found in the thanks of the republic they died to save. I pray that our Heavenly Father may assuage the anguish of your bereavement, and leave you only the cherished memory of the loved and lost, and the solemn pride that must be yours to have laid so costly a sacrifice upon the altar of freedom.*
>
> Yours very sincerely and respectfully,
A. Lincoln

When in 1914 the ambassador to Great Britain Walter H. Page wrote to his friend, President Woodrow Wilson, upon the death of Mrs. Wilson, he reflected a far different relationship:

> *My dear Wilson:*
>
> *There is nothing that even your oldest and nearest friends can say—words fail in the face of a bereavement like this. But I can't resist the impulse to write how deeply I feel for you.*
>
> *You would be touched if I could tell you the number of good men and women who every hour of the day and night have expressed to me the grief with which they heard the sad news—men and women who never saw you, from King down to the English messenger in our embassy . . .*

*But, my dear friend, it hits us hardest who have known you
longest and love you most and who wish for you now all possible
strength, in this sad, sad hour of the world when, more than any
other man in the world, you are most needed—all possible
strength to you. If the deep sympathy of all your friends, known
and unknown to you, can help to support you and to keep your
high spirit and courage up, you have it in most abundant
measure.*

Mrs. Page and I grieve with you and hope for you to the utmost.

Yours with affectionate sympathy,

What Should You Say?

MAKE A FEW NOTATIONS to yourself before you start. Your very
first sentence should acknowledge the loss and name the deceased, if
possible. Your first thoughts are often your best, like the honesty of
these first sentences of notes of sympathy by the following persons,
some of them famous:

F. Scott Fitzgerald: *"I can't tell you how I feel about Monsignor
Fay's death—He was the best friend I had in the world. . . ."*

Lewis Carroll [Charles Dodgson] to his brother and sister-in-
law: *"I must write one line to tell you how truly I feel, with you
and for you, in this sorrow that has come upon you. . . ."*

Henry James to Robert Louis Stevenson's widow: *"What can I
say to you that will not seem cruelly irrelevant and vain? . . ."*

George Eliot: *"I believe you are one of the few who can understand that in certain crises direct expression of sympathy is the
least possible to those who most feel sympathy. . . ."*

But you don't have to be a famous writer. Start simply:

*I read in today's newspaper of the death of your beloved Jack, and
wanted you to know how very sorry I am. . . .*

*It is with a very sad heart that I send my condolences to you upon
the loss of your dear friend, Max . . .*

*Since I heard the news yesterday of the passing of Henry, my
thoughts have been filled with you and your loss . . .*

*I don't have words to express how very sorry I was to learn you lost
your beloved baby, Isabella . . .*

Remember that you cannot change the fact that someone has
died, or that someone is suffering. But you *can* convey that you are
sorry. And that you care. A written note can be an embrace.
Although words seem inadequate in the face of grief, they are a
start. Written words can carry the weight of caring and comfort.
They can be returned to over and over again.

To Whom Are You Writing?

YOUR NEXT SENTENCE WILL be based upon your relationship
with the grieving and the deceased. If you know the grieving, and
didn't know the deceased well, address the loss of the bereaved:

I know how close you and Madison were . . .

*I remember how frequently you spoke of your father and his great
"down-home" wisdom . . .*

Knowing you as I do, I know your mother must have been a wonderful woman . . .

There is no need to pretend a Utopian relationship existed between the grieving and the deceased if it did not. Focus on the grieving person and allude to the imperfection:

I know you put forth a tremendous effort to keep your relationship with your sister positive . . .

I remember all the times you rushed home from work to attend to your mother's needs . . .

No one could have been more caring than you were during Rickie's long illness . . .

Share an Honoring Memory

IF YOU KNEW THE DECEASED, this is the time to honor her or him by sharing a positive memory. People who have just lost loved ones often fear their loved ones he will be forgotten. A friend whose mentally ill son committed suicide craved details of his life from all his son's friends. The notes they wrote, he said, "allowed me to embrace him again and again." A memory or more about the deceased anchors your note with something the grieving can return to time after time. Make it as specific as possible. This same friend said he was comforted by stories of what his son meant to classmates in high school before he became ill, by tales of his son's great sportsmanship and his swimming skills, even by details of how he'd helped friends out of several scrapes. Whatever fond memory you have, share it:

I remember David was always the leader of our group when we'd get together for a pick-up game of basketball. What a great hook shot he had! . . .

I've never known a kinder person than Hillary. I remember when she stopped on the street to talk to a woman panhandling, and although we were late for our meeting, she went and bought the woman a sandwich . . .

The sun never set on your father's anger. I'll never forget that summer evening fishing out on the pier when he got a bit impatient with us. He said, "Now girls, the sun is going down and before it does I have some unfinished dust from the day I need to attend to" . . .

I can never think of your dad without the mental picture of his great down-the-line backhand, and that look of satisfaction on his face when the ball would zip by me . . .

When You Don't Know the Deceased Well

FOR COLLEAGUES, BUSINESS ASSOCIATES, people you know only casually, and strangers, your language will usually be a bit more formal and general. A short note of a few sentences is fine, as are a several lines written in a sympathy card.

Yes, strangers. Sometimes there's a stirring in your heart that needs to find expression, and that's what you need to listen to. Many of the letters and notes received by the parents of the teens killed at Columbine High School in Colorado were from strangers. They came in by the thousands.

Are There Special Circumstances?

DEATH OUT OF THE natural order—when a parent must bury a child, when an infant dies before birth or at a very young age, or when someone in the prime of life and seemingly the peak of health dies suddenly—compounds the sorrow. There truly are no adequate words at such a time. Sudden death means no goodbye. Death from AIDS, cancer, suicide, a fatal disease, or murder can leave mourners with an added burden of a social stigma or guilt.

Reach down into your heart and write. There is a touchstone in all of us that allows us to be honest and genuine, and to offer solace:

I cannot imagine the sorrow you are experiencing . . .

What can bring comfort at such a time? Please know you are on my heart and mind . . .

Please know there are many here who care that you are suffering. Though we can't know your pain, our thoughts and prayers are with you . . .

I don't have any words to match such a loss. If it would help to talk, I am a good listener . . .

I don't pretend to understand the sadness you are feeling at losing April . . .

A Few Choice Words

SOMETIMES THE WORDS YOU feel have already been written by someone. Use them. Quote the words and credit the author. Some of the best words for those of the Jewish or Christian faiths come from the Old Testament, especially the Psalms. There are also many poems, prose, and lines from plays that may be used. But don't include a religious message unless you know the feelings of the mourner.

Don't lapse into a misguided effort to empathize by offering such words as, "I know how you feel." And don't make your note about your grief: "When my aunt died. . . ." Platitudes, no matter how well intended, aren't comforting. Mourners are usually not comforted by words like "He's in a far better place now," or "At least she's not suffering anymore."

Offer Help

DONNA, WHOSE HUSBAND DIED of a heart attack, was faced with grieving at a sudden loss, taking care of her husband's critically ill mother, managing a full-time job, and caring for her two small children. "Specific offers of help were best," she said, "because I could say yes or no, but beyond that I was overtaxed." Coworkers showed up and brought activities for the children, daycare workers kept the kids after hours, a friend of her husband's asked if he might take her son on regular outings. "And those who just came to be with me were wonderful."

Make your offer of help specific and tailored to the needs and desires of the grieving. A call, an e-mail, or checking in with someone very close to the mourner can give you the answers about what would be most helpful.

Write Again

SPECIAL DAYS AFTER A death like wedding anniversaries, birth-days, and holidays often make the grieving person feel the loss anew. Write again at such times, and open your heart:

I know today would have been your tenth wedding anniversary, and I just wanted you to know my thoughts are with you today . . .

The anniversary of Rachel's death always brings several days of special thoughts about her. How I miss her! Remember the day we took the picnic to the sand dunes, and the gust of wind came up and blew sand all over her made-from-scratch angel food cake covered with her special seven-minute frosting?

She only laughed that wonderful, bubbling laugh, and said, "Well, there will be a few less calories after you scrape off that gritty icing." How thankful I am that we got to love her . . .

I know Timmy's birthday preparations always bring back a flood of memories of the onset of Kirk's illness. I can still see his face on that last Saturday, the sun on his bright cheeks, blonde hair flying, as he and Timmy took off down the beach with that kite . . .

PART FOUR

Notes of Refusal, Apology, and Forgiveness

22

Refusals

> *May 25, 1944*
>
> *Dear _____:*
>
> *You do write with such power, such expressiveness, that it is too bad you should not be published . . .*
>
> *That is just my point. The tragedy of man is that reason and tempered wisdom are always, throughout man's history, overcome by passion and ungoverned emotion . . .*
>
> *Ever sincerely yours,*
—Refusal letter to a would-be novelist by
Maxwell E. Perkins, editor

REFUSAL IS A MATTER of both art and grace. It's very important to know yourself, and to make your answer of refusal firm, but kind. And timely. Your refusal will generally have two jobs to do: say "no," and still promote goodwill.

Because I so hate saying "no" to a request, I can find myself launching a litany of reasons (some would say excuses) as to why I can't do a requested deed. But the truth is, a request is just that; it's not to be confused with a demand. I, and you, owe no explanation for saying "no."

Start with a Positive Statement

IT'S OFTEN MOST TACTFUL, especially when something is strictly a business matter with someone you don't know well, to start with a positive statement:

> *It is very flattering to receive a nomination to the board. Many very talented writers have served on this esteemed panel. I cannot, however, accept the nomination . . .*

> *I understand your rationale that I'm a Midwesterner at heart, and it would, therefore, make great sales sense for me to head the new office, but I cannot consider it . . .*

> *Your offer is very generous, but I must say no.*

Say "No" with Conviction

THE BIGGEST AND MOST powerful kindness you can perform is to leave no room for the requester to believe you can be persuaded to say "yes."

You may at first think just saying "no" is brutal, too harsh, and needs to be softened a bit. It doesn't. It is the kindest stroke. Here's an all-too-common, afraid-to-say-no response: A friend was asked to judge the category of nonfiction books published for an annual regional competition. She knew she was going to be very busy finishing her own book manuscript and conducting a conference, but she didn't, "couldn't," say no. Instead, she responded, "I might be able to do that . . ." and went into a detailed list of her many commitments. When she waffled, the requester jumped in with additional enticement, "I'm sure there won't be that many entries." My friend continued to hesitate, then said, "Oh, maybe I can do it." Her answer was taken, of course, as a "yes," and the requester looked no further for a judge to fill the spot.

Weeks later, several large cartons of books arrived at the reluctant volunteer's door. She was a bit overwhelmed, but took the books in and placed them in her study for several more weeks. Two weeks before she was to have completed the judging, she called the requester in a panic and said, "I can't do this." The refusal at this last hour left the contest in disarray, and the person in charge without a judge for this category.

Had my friend said "no" immediately in a written note, she would have found it possible to do so without waffling, and it would have allowed the requester time to find a proper, qualified judge. The requester would not have spent valuable time assuming the judging was all handled, and my friend's reputation with this group would have maintained its sterling glimmer. Her lack of a proper "no" left her reputation tarnished. The point is, you must be certain of your "no," and say it with conviction.

Here's another fine example of how legendary editor Max Perkins handled it:

Feb. 9, 1945

Dear Mr. Cowden:

I fully appreciate the compliment of being asked to be one of the judges of the Hopwood fiction contest, but I must, with deep regret, decline. It is my conviction that an editor should be even more obscure than a child, who should be seen. The editor should be neither seen nor heard, or so I think. And so I have made it a rule to do nothing but the regular editorial work, and not to speak, or lecture, or act as a judge, or to take on anything on the outside, even when greatly tempted, as now.

Ever sincerely yours,
[Maxwell E. Perkins]

Refusing a Friend

WHEN YOUR REFUSAL NOTE is being written to someone you know well, and the need to refuse is painful, the stakes are much higher. Your solid resolve is now imperative. In this case you may know that the polite ploy of first making a positive statement can be seen as rude, even insulting. When you know the person well, just say:

> *Jack, You know me well, and you know if I could coach this season I would. But I can't.*

> *It pains me to refuse, but I must.*

> *Saying "no" in this case is very difficult, but that has to be my answer.*

You *don't* need to explain your refusal. A request is neither a command nor a demand, and that's important to remember. In fact, your explanation may be viewed as an invitation to try to convince you. It opens the door to efforts to change your mind.

Do reply promptly; it will cause less disappointment and allow the requester time to make another arrangement.

When to Explain

YOU MAY *WANT* TO explain if the request comes from a close friend or relative. It might be seen rude *not* to. When your refusal comes after an initial "yes," or when your "no" comes after you allowed the other person to expend effort on your behalf, you certainly *owe* an explanation—plus your assistance in finding a replacement, plus an apology. If a realtor friend has done some research on homes for you, and you refuse to spend a Saturday looking at the homes he's located, you owe him a pretty substantial explanation: "Conan, We really appreciate your running the computer search for us, but after looking at all the numbers, we have decided that we will not be able to move into that neighborhood after all. Prices have just gone beyond our reach . . ."

Offer an explanation in tune with your heart, and in consideration of the person you're writing to. It should still be firm, direct, and conclusive, so you don't seem to be inviting negotiations or a debate. Don't say, for example, "Keep me in mind if you can't find someone else," "I would so love to help out another time," or "I feel so badly about being unable to do it," unless you mean it. These tags mark you for the next request, and if that isn't your desire, don't add them. Make your statement brief and final:

> . . . *I will be out of town that weekend, and unable to lend a hand . . .*

> . . . *I have a conflict on that date, I'm scheduled to be . . .*

> . . . *Perhaps at some later time I'll explain my refusal . . .*

How to End

END ON A NOTE of goodwill:

. . . *We are still sisters-in-law, and you have all my best wishes.*

. . . *I regret I can only support you indirectly, but that I do with good thoughts and good wishes, and the occasional recommendation of your company for consulting work.*

. . . *I will continue to support the organization financially, and I look forward to seeing the next progress report. You are doing good and needed work.*

. . . *What I can do is help with the expenses, and I've enclosed a check.*

. . . *Again, I am honored to be considered, and I eagerly await the next report from the board. This should be an exciting year for the organization.*

To H. G. Leach   *52 Tavistock Square, W.C.I*

Oct 14th 1925
Dear Mr. Leach,
    My husband has told me of his talk with you, and I have now had a letter from the Forum office. It is very good of you to ask me to submit another story for your consideration, but I feel that it would only be a waste of your time. The stories I have at present are much in the same style as The New Dress *and are open to the same objections. But if at any time I should write*

anything which appears more likely to suit you, I shall have great pleasure in submitting it. I much regret that illness prevented me from seeing you.

Yours sincerely
Virginia Woolf

23

An apology has the power to generate forgiveness.
—DR. AARON LAZARE, *Chancellor/Dean
University of Massachusetts Medical Center*

APOLOGIZING ISN'T FOR sissies. In fact, it's an act of moral courage. To do it well, we must be secure in who we are, because apologizing requires that we admit such things as weakness, failure, and wrongdoing. For our apology to work, it must be well thought out, clearly stated, and heartfelt.

On Christmas day, a young adult in a pique over the behavior of a stepparent wailed, ". . . and don't give me one of your lame apologies. I don't want to hear it. You're not sorry, and everyone knows it." That, of course, didn't add to the holiday harmony; but neither, I suspect, would have the referenced "apology." I think we all suspect the "easy" apology: it sounds and feels false. Dr. Aaron Lazare, who has studied the subject extensively, has named the entire category of easy, ego-saving efforts "pseudoapologies." Do any of these apologies that *really aren't* sound familiar?

Sorry.
This is a perfunctory word offered to close the subject; or as a demand to the offended person: now forget it, and let's move

on. It doesn't state what you're sorry for, why you did what you did, or if you intend to do it again. The word "sorry" itself doesn't necessarily mean "I apologize." It may mean, "I'm sorry that it happened"; or it may even mean, "I'm sorry I got caught," or even "I'm sorry you're making an issue of it."

I'm sorry you're upset.
This statement says the offender is accepting no responsibility. Instead, she's placing the responsibility squarely back on the offended person by defining the problem in terms of the offended person's emotions, not in terms of her actions.

You know I didn't mean it. You're trying to make me feel guilty.
Instead of accepting responsibility, this attempts to make the offended person feel responsible for the offender's guilt.

I regard you as a friend. I would never intentionally hurt you.
The offended person is left to conclude it is her fault she feels injured: either the offended person is too thin-skinned, or she has misunderstood, or attributed a mean motive where there was none.

I wouldn't have done it if you hadn't . . .
This excuse, too, is aimed at escaping responsibility, and placing guilt on the offended.

We all know that failed apologies—those not given, botched, or not accepted—can produce ruptured relationships, life-long grudges, and embittered efforts at vengeance. In confessing that, at one time or another, she had used all of these statements, the step-parent said, "I guess I fear I'll be thought of as weak, or I'll be overcome with my feelings of shame; or the person I've offended will require that I jump through a lot of hoops to make something right . . . Or maybe all of these."

The truth is that apologizing—genuinely meaning and saying, "I'm sorry"—isn't easy. It chafes the ego and can rub a blister over our pride. The other truth is that *pseudoapologies don't work because they won't clear your conscience.*

When You've Offended Someone

A *GENUINE* APOLOGY is a solution. It can eliminate the problem, disperse that gathering cloud of bad weather between you and the offended person, and restore your relationship by opening the door to forgiveness and healing for both yourself and the offended person. It can also restore the offended person's belief in you, and allow her to once again embrace your relationship.

But it must be said that relationships are messy, and the process of apologizing for a personal offense is a dynamic transaction between two people. There's no guarantee of a particular outcome, and sometimes apologizing takes negotiation.

Think of apologizing as cleaning your slate; paying a bill

Written apologies benefit both the maker of the apology and the receiver. Going deep within ourselves and processing, or working through the offense, gives our words the weight they require. It also demonstrates our sincerity to the offended person.

If you've offended someone, the process must start with a real desire on your part to right a wrong. (And it also requires that the wounded person place a higher value on your relationship than on nurturing a wound.) When I realized I'd forgotten about a dinner at a friend's house, I immediately called and expressed how sorry I was, then I sat down and wrote this note:

> *Dear Perry, I can offer no other explanation than that I had a complete "blond moment." After going out for an evening walk, I suddenly remembered I was supposed to be at your dinner party experiencing, with the rest of the club-member guests, one of your culinary appetizer delights.*
>
> *I apologize, profusely.*
>
> *Since I know white tulips are your favorite (and I'm not at this moment), I hope you'll accept these as a token of my contrition. I'll even go brunette if you'll forgive me. (Well, maybe auburn.)*

There are, of course, offenses of *omission* and *commission*. Apologizing for an *intentional* personal offense that has attacked and lowered the other person's self-image and has created a real social wound is more difficult; although you'll usually do it verbally first, a written apology is often needed, too. Here's one Lewis Carroll (Charles L. Dodgson) wrote for something as simple as not greeting someone:

> Christ Church, Oxford
> June 22, 1893
>
> Dear Lord Rosebery,
>   *I will not trespass on your fully-occupied time with more than a few words. We met, in the Quadrangle yesterday, almost face to face, and I would certainly have taken the initiative in greeting you, as one of our guests known to me, but that I fancied that it*

*rested with you, as my superior in rank, to speak first. It has since
occurred to me that perhaps you thought it rested with me, as the
senior. My reason for writing now is that I fear you may have
thought that my motive for silence was an unfriendly recollection
of a difficulty that arose, many years ago, between us as lecturer
and pupil.*

*Pray accept my assurance that this is not so. I have no
unfriendly feeling whatever, as to an incident which was fully
settled at the time, towards you: and I sincerely trust you have
none towards me.*

*Should chance ever bring us together again, I earnestly hope
we may meet as if no such incident had ever occurred,*

Sincerely yours,
Charles L. Dodgson

Consider the sincerity of this apology of Winston Churchill to
his wife, Clementine:

O From WSC   Chequers
25 August 1954

My darling beloved Clemmie,

*Do forgive me for my lapse this morning, I was preoccupied
with dictating a message to Ike. I only wanted the Portal [Jane]
not to go back to the Office but wait in the next room while we
had a talk. I was enraptured by yr lovely smile of greeting,
& longing to kiss you. All this I spoiled by my clumsiness &
gaucherie. I cherish your morning comings & I beseech you to be
noble & generous as you always are to your thoroughly penitent &
much ashamed, but loving, & hopeful*

W

P.S. You have been so bright & splendid here and I have thanked God to see you much stronger. I will try to do better.

What Makes an Apology Work?

OFFENDING SOMEONE ROBS a person of power. Apologizing gives that power back. It's this exchange that allows the healing process to begin.

Properly time your apology. For a single, minor offense, like failing to introduce someone or being late for a meeting, apologizing immediately in the conversation can prevent a small offense from becoming a larger one. But when a serious personal offense has been committed, like making a disparaging comment or lying to someone, it may take time for both the offender and the offended to integrate the impact of the offense before an apology can be made or received. And it's often best to put it in writing.

The apology must match or measure up to the offense and its consequences. Don't expect that after years of neglect, for example, a simple "I'm sorry" will set things right. Whether the offense was minor or major, and whether you first offer a verbal apology, follow these five basic steps in writing your note:

1. Acknowledge and accept responsibility for the offense. This step has three parts: (1) acknowledge you have violated a moral code—standards such as honesty, fairness, faithfulness, thoughtfulness, sensitivity, or loyalty; (2) accept responsibility without excusing yourself; and (3) acknowledge and come to understand the impact of the offense on the other person.

Start by naming the offense, and be very specific:

Jodie, I promised you I'd be home at five o'clock sharp, and I didn't show . . .

I know that we promised we'd be each other's maid of honor at our weddings, and I broke my promise.

I need to apologize. I took credit for the wonderful job you did . . .

Or, start simply: "I'm truly sorry . . . ," "Please forgive me . . . ," "I must accept the responsibility for . . . ," "I am at fault . . . ," "It was my mistake . . . ," "I was wrong . . . ," "I must correct the . . . ," "Please accept my apology for . . ."

Connect the injury to the person. State how you believe the offense injured the person's self-image (the story we believe about ourselves). This validates the person's feelings of being ignored, belittled, betrayed, humiliated, or whatever, and it demonstrates that you understand the nature of your wrongdoing, and the impact it had on her. Understanding the other person's feelings helps you take responsibility for the consequences of your behavior:

. . . I know this must have hurt you very much.

. . . I know you've looked forward to being in my wedding since we were ten and twelve.

. . . I know how hard you worked on that brochure, and how much pride you take in it.

Offer to listen to how she felt injured:

. . . That's what I think, but I'd like to have you tell me how you felt, if you would . . .

. . . I'm willing to listen. Please tell me how I hurt you, if you will . . .

. . . Please talk to me about your feelings.

2. Explain. State *why* you committed the offense, or give the extenuating circumstances, if they exist; *but don't manufacture an excuse*:

. . . I left my office on time but there was an accident at 64th and Broadway that held up traffic for twenty-five minutes.

. . . I used the official directory to check the spelling of your name, and it is misspelled there . . .

. . . you weren't invited because Jane and I divided the list of names, and the only L, you, got dropped because each of us thought it was on the other's list.

By giving a factual explanation, you can help to protect the offended person's self-concept. It tells her, for example, that you realize her time is important and you value it, or that it was simply a faultless error. It also protects your self-concept: you are the kind of person who intends and tries to keep your commitments. Making up a traffic story to cover up for the fact that you thoughtlessly made three extra phone calls instead of leaving your office on time, however, will smell like the manufactured excuse it is. But more important, it won't clear your conscience.

3. Communicate your regret. This is the key ingredient, and must come from the heart—especially in offenses of *commission*. It should contain a statement of your emotions of anxiety, sadness, guilt, and shame. *Anxiety* and *sadness* convey anticipation of the loss of the relationship; *guilt* expresses distress over causing damage to the offended person; and *shame* expresses your distress in failing to live up to your own standards:

> . . . *I feel horrible about leaving you in the lurch. I acted irresponsibly . . .*

> . . . *I have no excuse. I admired the job you did on the brochure, and secretly wished that I had done it. When Vickie assumed I had done it, I was thrilled. I just let her heap on the praise, and while I realized I should correct her, I didn't. The truth is, I have always envied your talent. It has taken me a while to wrestle with myself about what I did. I'm truly ashamed. . . .*

State your decision to change your future behavior. The origin of the word *repent* means to change directions. If this were to happen again, you would act differently. You are repudiating or denouncing the act:

> . . . *I'm going to try very hard not to do this again. In the future, I resolve to keep my promises to you firmly in mind. And my telephone with me . . .*

> . . . *In addition to calling everyone who was at the meeting and telling them I falsely took credit for your work, I have written a piece for the newsletter expressing how thankful we are for your outstanding work. I promise I'll never do anything like this again . . .*

4. Make reparations. The offense creates a debt which needs to be repaid. Reparations are often symbolic, the apology being part or all of the repayment. But reparation also means that, in addition to apologizing, you make things *whole*, you even the score, you restore any harm you've done—like having an item you've broken properly fixed or replaced.

Here's an apology where making whole meant also apologizing to two other people who overheard an offending comment:

> *Dear Adrian,*
>
> *She who speaks first, and thinks later, is destined to a future riddled with the pain and embarrassment of making many apologies. And that, of course, is the reason I am making this one to you. It was wrong of me to say I wouldn't attend your party if it was going to be held at The York. I realize that now, and am chastened. Please forgive me for my loutish comment. I'm contacting both Georgia and Aubrey to apologize, too, as I'm sure they overheard.*
>
> *I'm thrilled to be invited (if I still am), and I look forward to attending a party in your honor. If given another chance, I promise to be a model guest.*
>
>

Your contrite friend,
Ginger
>

For such major offenses of *commission* as infidelity, chronic alcoholism, or abuse, a very strict plan for change must be part of the apology. Restoring such a fractured relationship will require an extensive step-by-step plan by the offender, and another by the offended. Both plans will need to enumerate what the offender needs to do, and precise behavior must be set down and then achieved before full forgiveness can take place.

5. Offer an Olive Branch. After the apology—having cleared your conscience and restored the relationship—closure may best be accomplished and rapport reestablished by making a gesture of friendship, or offering communication on an unrelated detail or a neutral subject. This can eliminate any remaining awkwardness. But don't rush it, as that could take away from the effectiveness of your apology. For minor offenses, this can easily be offered at the time of your apology, and as part of it. This can also help reestablish a "naturalness" between you and the offended person.

Here's how one sister apologized and offered recompense:

My Dearest Karen,

I've received your letter asking me for an apology. I've had a chance to think about it, and I feel horrible. Yes, you're right, I broke a sacred promise to be in your wedding. Karen, I love you very much, yet I've hurt you deeply, and I'm ashamed of myself. I can only say I was angry, as you know, because Mom gave you the ruby brooch, and I took my anger out on you. Please forgive me. (I've talked with Mom and have now reconciled the matter.)

Yes, I do understand that you feel marginalized by my actions. I can't, of course, turn back the clock and now be your maid of honor, and I will always regret that. But I'm going to try very hard not to hurt you ever again.

I know it isn't the same as being in your wedding, but I'd like to try to make amends by hosting a reception for you and Terry in San Francisco for your friends here who couldn't attend the wedding. Please allow me to do this. I'm thinking of about twenty people for a reception at the club, or in Napa Valley at Crystals, after you two return from your honeymoon. I hope you and Terry will let me do this as a token of my contrition and my love, and best wishes for your new life together.

With love always,
Michelle

Remember, an apology demonstrates strength of character. It takes courage. It says you are committed to a high moral code. It also says you are committed to your relationship, and it opens the door for transforming healing to take place. Apologizing says that although you make mistakes and have weaknesses, you are a strong and good person.

When You've Been Offended

No man can tell another his faults so as to benefit him, unless he loves him.
—HENRY WARD BEECHER,
Proverbs from Plymouth Pulpit (1887)

IT'S EASIER TO REACT with anger, or perhaps even sever a relationship entirely, than it is to ask for an apology. But if you've been offended and you want to heal and restore a relationship, *you* may need to initiate the forgiveness process by asking for an apology. It's difficult because you're already feeling wounded, and you won't want to discuss your pain and make yourself even more vulnerable.

If you're angry before you begin writing, give yourself a little time to reflect or cool off. It's often helpful to first write out your anger in a note to yourself, read it through, then tear it into pieces and throw it away. After a few hours, or overnight, you may see things more objectively and be able to express yourself better, without undue anger.

Writing a personal note allows you to absorb and work through the offense; and reading it allows the offender to reflect and process what she did and how it affected you. Using a written note has the added advantages of avoiding a confrontation, initiating a defensive reaction, or prompting an angry exchange.

Writing about how you *feel* reduces the chance your statement will be considered a counterattack. Start with something like:

> *I was very hurt by your statements about my religious beliefs. Not only did they offend me, they were inaccurate . . .*

> *I was very troubled by your statement that ridiculed the new signage. I felt you directly insulted my efforts and overlooked the fact that you were chairing the project . . .*

> *The fact that you forwarded my e-mail containing my short story to several friends, without asking me and getting my permission, shocked me. And I must also tell you that it violates copyright law . . .*

Add some explanation, and if needed, ask for negotiation: "*. . . I value our friendship, and that's why I would like to resolve this . . . ,*" "*. . . Would you think about this, and discuss it with me . . . ,*" or, "*. . . I'm not asking for your response right now. I suggest we talk about this next week . . .*" Don't give up easily if you value the relationship. Exert every effort to negotiate and work through the apology process to its healing end. And be open to hearing the other person's point of view.

If the offense was clear-cut and requires no negotiation, you may want to conclude: "*. . . I believe you owe me an apology, but I'd like to discuss the matter and learn how this happened, in case I have misinterpreted something . . .*".

If the offender doesn't apologize and won't discuss the offense and try to work it out, you may decide to discontinue the relationship. The most common reasons people don't apologize are because of pride (fear of shame), egocentricity, fear of the offended person's response, and requirements to make amends.

Your responsibility when you've been offended is to act honorably, with respect, fairness, and compassion. If you have, don't fault yourself.

And, as if our own human frailties weren't enough, now we have the added pressure of living in a litigious society, which warns us not to say things that could make us legally culpable. I must caution you here, too, that when your apology is legally actionable it's wise to first ask your lawyer about what you write, and keep a copy.

The Steps of Apology

- Start with a heartfelt desire to clear your conscience.
- Take responsibility and acknowledge how you offended the other person.
- Explain.
- Say you're sorry.
- Repair the damage.
- Offer an olive branch.

24

Forgiveness

We all like to forgive, and we all love best not those who offend us least, nor those who have done most for us, but those who make it most easy for us to forgive them.

—SAMUEL BUTLER

A LETTER TO WINSTON CHURCHILL from his wife, Clementine:

O From CSC   *10 Downing Street*
27 June 1940

My Darling,
    I hope you will forgive me if I tell you something that I feel you ought to know.
    One of the men in your entourage (a devoted friend) has been to me & told me that there is a danger of your being generally disliked by your colleagues & subordinates because of your rough sarcastic & overbearing manner—It seems your Private Secretaries have agreed to behave like schoolboys & 'take what's coming to them' & then escape out of your presence shrugging their shoulders—Higher up, if an idea is suggested (say at a conference) you are supposed to be so contemptuous that presently no ideas, good or bad, will be forthcoming. I was astonished & upset because in all these years I have been accustomed to all those who have worked

with & under you, loving you—I said this & I was told 'No doubt it's the strain'—

My Darling Winston—I must confess that I have noticed a deterioration in your manner; & you are not so kind as you used to be . . .

. . . I cannot bear that those who serve the Country & yourself should not love you as well as admire and respect you—

Besides you won't get the best results by irascibility & rudeness. They will breed either dislike or a slave mentality—(Rebellion in War time being out of the question!)

> *Please forgive your loving devoted & watchful*
> *Clemmie*

I wrote this at Chequers last Sunday, tore it up, but here it is now.

The book *Winston and Clementine: The Personal Letters of the Churchills* tells us:

No answer exists to Clementine's letter: perhaps they spoke. But Winston surely took it to heart: for although during the years of his greatest power he could undoubtedly be formidable and unreasonable, many of the people who served him at all levels in those dire years have put on record not only their admiration for him as a chief, but also their love for a warm and endearing human being.

If Winston Churchill had written a note of response to his wife, I would like to think it may have said something like this:

My Dearest Clemmie,

Not only do I forgive you, I must thank you with all of my heart for your love and courage and unfailing support in pointing out my failures with such kindness. Certainly you are correct in doing so, and I am grateful.

It is I, of course, who must apologize to you, and indeed to each of those in my entourage, for my "rough sarcastic and over-bearing manner." And it is I who must tell you, and each of them, that I am sorry for my irascibility and rudeness. I can only plead for your continued kindness and understanding during these dire and trying days as I endeavor to conduct myself with improved comportment.

I am your devoted loving husband

W

To forgive requires a real change of heart. After all, you have been wounded. When you've been injured by someone (see chapter 23, Apology), you will likely react in one of four ways: (1) you will express your anger; (2) you will deny your anger, insisting everything is fine; (3) you'll pretend you're not angry at all, while plotting revenge; or (4) you will forgive the person who injured you.

For a brief season after an injury, the anger you feel toward your offender is a good-feeling energizer. But if you allow it to fester, it will destroy your positive connection with the person who hurt you. And at the same time, intense anger and resentment can begin to gnaw away at *you*, eroding your joy and producing internal stress and anxiety. You may begin to feel a heavy sadness and a depression. You may realize that your anger has taken on a life of its own, and it has made you a prisoner of the past.

You may find yourself becoming more cynical, blaming others for your problems. And you may also find that your path to forgiveness is blocked and you have kissed goodbye your relationship with this person who offended you.

If left unresolved, you may even notice your other relationships start to suffer, as your negative emotions limit your ability to love, and your anger spills into your relationships with people who don't deserve it. *You've become the offender.* You've *displaced* your anger onto someone entirely undeserving of it.

Discovering Forgiveness

FORGIVENESS CAN ELIMINATE ANGER, restore your good self-image and hope, and reduce both anxiety and depression. It is important, though, to dispel any misconceptions you may have about forgiveness.

Forgiving is canceling a debt owed to you. It is a gift you decide to give the person who hurt you.

What Forgiveness Is NOT

Forgiving *is not*:

Forgetting. You'll always remember the injury you suffered.

Reconciling. In fact, when a very serious offense is involved, like incest or physical abuse, reconciling isn't even wise until many other steps have been completed. The offender may have to go to jail and undergo extensive therapy.

Condoning, excusing, or pardoning. The offender doesn't get away scot-free, she is still responsible for her misdeed.

Weakness. It doesn't mean you have become a patsy. Forgiving is a great act of courage.

Power. You aren't playing God.

There are several other important things to know about forgiveness: (1) *It doesn't usually occur quickly.* It often takes time. (2) *It's a private act* which takes place in your heart. You can forgive even without the offender knowing; even when the offender doesn't repent, atone, or apologize. (3) *It takes real commitment from you, the forgiver.*

There are a number of reasons besides your belief that holding onto your anger is morally wrong that may compel you to write a note of forgiveness. In forgiving, *you* will receive: (1) relief from your inner pain; and (2) relief for other loved ones your anger is hurting. You may also (3) restore social harmony; and (4) reconcile with the offender.

Start with a Decision

YOU MUST FIRST DECIDE to forgive. This usually involves a number of steps:

1. Examine your anger and how it is affecting you, and realize it isn't your friend.

2. *Choose* forgiveness and *commit* to it as the path you'll take. (This also means you give up revenge.)

3. Begin *thinking* about the offender from a new perspective. Think about her as a vulnerable human being with weaknesses and strengths just like yours. In this act of "reframing" it may help to ask yourself: What was it like for her at the time of the offense? Was she under extreme stress? Are there other reasons why she did what she did?

4. *Empathize.* Try to *feel* how she must have felt. Stepping into the offender's shoes will help you develop the necessary feelings of tenderness required to effect true forgiveness.

5. Accept what has happened, and absorb the pain without tossing it back at the person who offended you, or displacing it onto other people.

6. Enjoy the byproducts of forgiveness: increased hopefulness, release from the bondage of anger, increased emotional strength and inner peace.

Think of writing your note of forgiveness as issuing a receipt for a debt paid.

Writing from Your Heart

WRITING A NOTE TELLING someone she is forgiven may not be appropriate unless she requests it.

To write your note to your offender, plain words are undoubtedly the best. Start with the simple fact:

I do forgive you . . .

Please know that you are forgiven . . .

I accept your apology, and I do forgive you . . .

You certainly have my forgiveness. It would be a pity to allow this to come between us . . .

I know you are sorry about this, and it cheers me to say I forgive you . . .

The Wonderful Paradox of Forgiveness

Forgiveness offers some wonderful paradoxes:

- even though you have every right to hold onto your anger against the person who wronged you, you choose to let it go;
- the person who offended you has no right to your gift of forgiveness, yet she gets it;
- the person who offended you doesn't benefit by your gift of forgiveness, yet *you* do. *You* are freed from the anger that chained you to her.

Next, you may want to demonstrate your empathy:

. . . Your explanation was very helpful. It opened my eyes to understanding the extreme stresses you were experiencing when . . .

. . . I now understand how this happened . . .

You may wish to conclude with a "clean slate" statement of reconciliation, and say something about your hope for a positive future relationship:

. . . I would like to suggest that in the future we avoid such possibilities for misunderstandings by . . .

. . . Our relationship is very important to me, and I commit to never allowing anything like this to come between us again . . .

. . . I value your friendship, and I will certainly take you at your word and discuss with you any behavior I find offensive. I request that you do the same with me . . .

In response to the dinner guest who apologizes in the note on page 217, the host may have decided to respond:

Dear Anna,

I accept your apology. (Certainly the white tulips helped assuage my anger. They are lovely.) You're forgiven; but I do, of course, regret that you missed my dinner party. We all missed you.

Yes, I understand the rare "blonde moment." I've had two myself, recently. (And I have no hair at all.) I completely forgot a dentist appointment on Tuesday, then a doctor's appointment on Wednesday—after both staffs called to remind me.

No, you're certainly not banished forever from the Fredrick dining table, but in the future I'll make a reminder call—that is, if I remember myself.

As always,
Perry

P.S. We all still love you blonde.

I like to imagine that Lord Rosebery, in replying to the note of apology written by Charles L. Dodgson (Lewis Carroll) on pages 217–218, wrote something like this:

My Dear Charles,

Certainly I bear you no ill will, or even a cross thought, con-

cerning the lack of greeting upon our chance meeting in the Quadrangle on 21 June, and I long ago forgave—alas have nearly forgotten, as well—the difficulty that once arose between us as lecturer and pupil.

In the hope that we may become good and true colleagues at Oxford in the future, may I suggest that we make a complete reconciliation by meeting to discuss any residual discomfort concerning that long-ago difficulty. It is my desire that we might henceforth enjoy an amicable and mutually rewarding relationship.

Would you dine with me at the Roundtable on 15 July at 7:00 P.M.? I look forward to receiving your note of acceptance.

Cordially yours,
Lord Rosebery

A sincere note of forgiveness from your heart has the power to heal and completely restore a relationship.

Selected Library

There may be times when you need just the right word, phrase, quotation, or form. You may find it in one of the following volumes.

Bartlett, John. *Bartlett's Familiar Quotations*, 16th Edition, Justin Kaplan, Editor. Boston: Little, Brown, 1992.

Cameron, Julia. *The Right to Write*. New York: Penguin Putnam, 1998.

Ehrlich, Eugene, and Marshall Debruhl, comps. *The International Thesaurus of Quotations*. New York: Harper Perennial, 1996.

Goldberg, Natalie. *Writing Down the Bones*. Boston: Shambhala Publications, Inc., 1986.

Lamb, Sandra E. *How to Write It*. Berkeley: Ten Speed Press, 1999.

Lewis, C. S. *A Grief Observed*. New York: HarperCollins, 2000.

Post, Peggy. *Emily Post's Etiquette*. 16th Edition. New York: HarperCollins, 1997.

Soames, Mary, ed. *Winston and Clementine: The Personal Letters of the Churchills*. New York: Houghton Mifflin Company, 1998.

Strunk, William, and E. B. White. *The Elements of Style*. Fourth Edition. Boston: Allyn and Bacon, 2000.

Taylor, Judy, ed. *Letters to Children from Beatrix Potter*. London: Penguin, 1992.

Theroux, Phyllis, ed. *The Book of Eulogies*. New York: Scribners, 1997.